# DON'T AWAKEN LOVE
# BEFORE THE TIME

Don't Awaken Love Before the Time
© 2003 By David A. Garcia
Printed in the United States of America

**_Ambassador Emerald International_**
427 Wade Hampton Boulevard
Greenville, S.C. 29609 U.S.A.

and

**_Ambassador Productions Ltd._**
Providence House
Ardenlee Street
Belfast BT6 8QJ, Northern Ireland

www.emeraldhouse.com

Cover design and page layout by A & E Media, Sam Laterza

**ISBN 1 889893 99 4**

# DON'T AWAKEN LOVE
# BEFORE THE TIME

### WHY YOUNG PEOPLE LOSE WHEN THEY DATE

## DAVID A. GARCIA

### AMBASSADOR
#### EMERALD INTERNATIONAL

GREENVILLE, SOUTH CAROLINA · BELFAST, NORTHERN IRELAND

# Acknowledgments

First of all I want to thank the Lord for giving me inspiration and compassion for the young people of today.

I would like to thank the following individuals for their help and support throughout the writing of this book:

To my wife, Nellie, for her support, encouragement and insights. To my children, Carissa and David. Thank you for being godly examples. Each of you are a special blessing from God.

To the entire staff and leadership at Brooksville Assembly of God. May God reward each of you for your faithful service and loving support.

To the entire Youth Ministry at Brooksville Assembly of God. The pastors, leaders and youth for supporting and embracing my belief in courtship.

To Charlotte Edwards and Fran Munoz for their invaluable help in typing of the manuscript.

To Bill and Patti Patrick for their encouragement and assistance.

Finally my heart-felt thanks to Dr. Sam Lowry and the Ambassador-Emerald publishing staff.

# TABLE OF CONTENTS

# CHAPTER 1
## Collision Course

A late night CNN report shows a police chase. Three police cruisers pursue four teenaged boys in a four-door sedan speeding recklessly through the streets of a large urban city. The roads are slippery after three days of continuous rain. The police have already warned them to pull over. What began as a night of joyriding and wild recklessness comes to a sudden end with a grinding head-on collision. There are three fatalities with one teen barely surviving.

What plan of action could have been used to stop the car and avoid this tragedy? Do you think that perhaps the police could have put up roadblocks? Or, as they do in many parts of the United States, could they have used road spikes to immediately blow out the tires of the speeding car? Or, as one group of teenagers once asked me, "Could they have shot out the tires?" One young girl suggested that the police should have even shot the driver! Although all of the aforementioned methods would have stopped the vehicle, the best course of action would have been to keep the car in the garage from the beginning.

There are millions of young people today who are taking a joy ride in a car called romance, enjoying themselves, and heading on a collision course with reality. What do cars and the subject of romance have in common?

First of all, both activities require rules and regulations. You don't just get into a car and disregard the rules. If you do, it is almost inevitable that you will eventually be involved in an accident with another motorist, collide with some other object, or worse yet, injure or kill a pedestrian. The same principle applies to romance. Certain rules and regulations must guide the relationship. Otherwise it is headed for a collision course.

Secondly, both activities require that we pick up passengers. We can readily see this with cars since their purpose is to transport not only the driver but other passengers as well. Thirdly, both require the operators to be old enough and mature enough to operate a vehicle, understand the rules of the road, and make wise decisions. This is especially true for the subject of romance. Here, too, you must be old enough, and you must understand the rules of life.

Sadly, many are entering romance before they know how to operate the vehicle. They awaken love before the right time. New drivers, 16 and 17 years old, have higher insurance rates when they first get their licenses. This is especially true in the case of male drivers. Why is this? It is because these drivers are higher risks. They may know how to move and operate a vehicle, but that doesn't make them wise drivers. Young drivers also are known to take far more risks than experienced drivers. Their tendency to drive at excessive speeds is a primary risk factor that puts them (and those around them) in unnecessary danger.

How does this apply to romance? You must know and follow the rules of the road in the area of romance (or more to the point, the rules of life).

- What are the rules of romance?
- Does the Word of God have anything to say about this subject?
- Why is it that so many young people are so quick to enter into relationships, speed up romance and finish in a head-on collision with sexual immorality, sexually transmitted diseases, unwanted pregnancies and even rape?

The answer to these questions is deceptively simple: romance is starting far too soon. No one in their right mind would ever give their third or fourth grader the keys to their car. That would result in an accident for sure. But at the same time, our third and fourth graders and in some cases even first and second graders are beginning to ask for the keys of romantic interest. Many young people today are actually awakening love before the time. This leads to a head-on collision of sexual experimentation and sexual immorality.

An excellent feature entitled "Teens and Sex" appeared in the May 27, 2002, issue of *US News and World Report*. It reported:

> "Kids from all walks of life are having sex at younger and younger ages. Nearly one in ten reports losing his or her virginity before the age of 13; a 15 percent increase since 1997 according to the Center for Disease Control and Prevention. Some 16 percent of high school sophomores have had four or more

sexual partners. One in four sexually active teens will contract a sexually transmitted disease or STD according to the Allan Guttmacher Institute. Despite a solid 20 percent decrease in the teen birth rate between 1991 and 1999, twenty percent of sexually active girls 15-19 get pregnant each year, according to the Henry J. Kaiser Family Foundation."

The report goes on to quote Lynn Ponton, a professor of psychiatry at the University of California, San Francisco, and the author of *Sex Lives of Teenagers*. She said that this early initiation into sexual behaviors is taking a toll on teens' mental health. "The result," she writes, "can be dependency on boyfriends and girlfriends, serious depression around breakups and cheating, lack of goals, all of these things at such young ages."

An article in the weekend edition of *USA Today* (March 15-17, 2002) reported, "The sexual revolution hits junior high. The kids are doing more than baring bellies. They're shocking adults with their anything goes behavior." The article continues:

"Researchers at Washington DC recently started a program to prevent early sexual activity. They planned to offer it to seventh graders, but after a pilot study, decided to target fifth graders because too many seventh graders were already having sex. Jo Mecham, a nurse at Bettendorf Iowa Middle School, says she overhears 'pretty explicit sexual talk from boys and girls in her conservative community. And, despite the dress code, girls come to class looking like bare bellied rock stars. They'll leave the house totally OK, and when they get to school they start disrobing.'"

The story goes on to give a report called "Sex by Age Fourteen" covering kids 15 and older who say they had engaged in intercourse by age 14! According to the report by Child Trends, a Washington research group, in 1988 eleven percent of the girls surveyed admitted they had engaged in sex by the age of 14, and twenty-one percent of the boys admitted the same. By 1995, the number of girls sexually active by age 14 rose to nineteen percent, with no change reported among the boys. The report also quoted another person saying almost fifty percent of the seventh and eighth graders at her school engaged in some kind of sex. A teacher said, "Youths are really getting involved in things a whole lot sooner than we thought."

According to a report in *US News & World Report* (May 27, 2002):

> "In 1999, the most recent year for which statistics are available, two thirds of graduating seniors and fifty percent of all high schoolers reported having engaged in intercourse, down over all from fifty-four percent of high schoolers in 1991. Yet the same report goes on to say that the reason for the downturn was that many young people are experimenting with other forms of sex that they do not consider "to be real sex."

In other words, our "dating system" (or what many young people call "going out") is putting millions of young people on a collision course with sexual immorality. Years from now, after bouncing from crash after crash, those victims are likely to career onto the ultimate collision course – divorce. As stated earlier, driving requires that you know the rules of the road. Are there rules of the road for romance? The answer is yes. They are found in the Word of God. The Bible gives us the absolute truths that we need to live our lives — especially in the realm of romance.

# CHAPTER 2
## You Can Be Absolutely Sure Of Only One Absolute

*A person's belief system is determined by what is perceived to be truth. The decisions a person makes and the actions a person takes are affected by his or her belief system.*

Have you ever been in a room when suddenly all the lights went out? What is the first thing you want to do? If you are like me, you generally move very slowly until you find a wall because it provides a sense of security (and because you find light switches on walls). Truth is like a wall that provides a secure boundary of what we believe to be truth. We need answers in this life, and young people are actively searching for the truth. Here's an important principle: *What a person believes to be truth will determine that person's belief system. That belief system, in turn, determines the person's decisions and actions.* It is, therefore, critically important that our decisions are based on absolute truths.

If truths are proven principles and doctrines by which individuals can know how to live, then they *cannot change* with different cultures, fads, or eras of history. This is extremely important because there are many voices seeking to influence a young person's decisions.

First, there is the voice of "self" which reflects the deep passions, desires, and wants of an individual. Is something—such as dating— "right" merely because it seems desirable and appears to be innocent? Can sexual immorality be justified by two individuals simply because they say that they love each other?

Second, there are the voices of "other people." These include the voices of parents, teachers, and other authorities who constantly mold what we believe to be truth.

Remember, your belief system and your values will help determine your decisions. Are the voices of other people reliable? Perhaps, but they may just as easily steer you the wrong way. You cannot just echo the excuse of choice for so many today, "Well, everybody's doing it and everybody's saying it. Therefore, it must be right."

The third voice comes from Satan. This fallen angel is very real, and he would have us believe everything that is opposed to God. His whole purpose is to destroy your eternal destiny and your eternal purposes in God. He will tell you everything that goes against God.

The fourth voice comes from God and His Word. The Bible will always steer you to the absolute truth. There are only two universal, absolute truths in this world. They are the Word of God and Jesus Christ.

*"All scripture is given by inspiration of God, and is profitable for doctrine, for reproof, for correction, for instruction in righteousness," II Timothy 3:16 (NKJV)*

*"Jesus said to him, 'I am the way, the truth, and the life. No one comes to the Father except through Me.'" John 14:6 9 (NKJV)*

Here Jesus clearly declares that He is truth. Notice that He does not merely preach truth, He *is* Truth. This is extremely important because our beliefs determine our values, and our values determine our decisions.

Our decisions will eventually determine our destiny. When it comes to the subject of dating and going out we have to allow God to determine our belief system. We must allow God's Word and Jesus Christ our Lord and Savior to determine our values, our decisions, and our destiny. We have to be aware that there is a subtle deception that has crawled into the church and, indeed, in most universities around the world since the early 1950's.

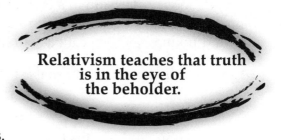

**Relativism teaches that truth is in the eye of the beholder.**

Authors Francis J. Beckwith and Gregory Koukl express concern with what they call "the death of truth" in their book *Relativism*. "We refer to the death of what the late Dr. Francis Shaeffer called "true truths," the extinction of the idea that any particular thing can be known for sure. Today, we've lost the confidence that statements of fact can ever be anything more than just opinions. We no longer know anything is certain beyond our subjective preferences. The word "true" now means true for me and nothing more. We have entered an era of dogmatic skepticism."

Relativism teaches that truth is in the eye of the beholder. In other words, if the person does not agree with what is being presented, he simply says "It's not relative to my life and, therefore, I do not have to obey or abide by its mandates." You see another byproduct of Relativism when you hear a talk show host ask, "Audience, do you agree with that?" If the crowd thunders a loud "no," then the contestant is told, "Well, the audience doesn't agree. Therefore, it must not be true."

According to the doctrines of Relativism, truth is in the hands of the majority and not those who have the truth. This philosophical system also claims that truth can change from one situation to another. In other words, one may feel right about a decision in a certain situation but is free to make a contrary decision if circumstances change. This way of thinking has been called "situation ethics."

Again, I will summarize the basic tenants of Relativism:

- No truth can be known for sure.
- Truth now means "it is true for me if it is relative to me."
- Truth can change from one situation to another depending upon your circumstances.
- Truth is in the hands of the majority. (Majority Rule)
- Truth changes from society to society. (What is true for one society may not be true for another if it is deemed appalling or unacceptable by that society.)

Can you see the immediate problems this causes when it comes to romance, going out, sexual purity, and morality? Relativism has caused many Christians to battle constantly with immorality. Many of them rationalize their sin, saying, "If you love me, you'll let me."

If a Christian takes a relativistic approach to going out and to romance, the end result will be compromise and what was referred to as a "head on collision" in Chapter 1. We need to return to the absolute truths of God's Word and Jesus Christ.

Does the Word of God say anything about dating or going out with somebody? The answer is "No." Well, you might ask, "Why does the Word of God not say anything about such an important subject?" The answer is simple. No one dated in the Bible, and no one "went out." Young people didn't hang out in the plaza drifting from one relationship to another to find out if they were "meant for each other." People simply did not practice dating or going out.

In fact, dating is a relatively new concept. It began in the early 1900's with the invention of the automobile. That is when young men started taking out young girls away from the authority of their parents; the erosion of the ethics of purity and morality began, and the divorce rate started rising.

Here is an important principle: *Bible principles produce Bible results.* Are there any Bible principles in the Word of God regarding romance? The answer is yes.

The first Bible principle for romance is revealed in the birth of Jesus:

"Now the birth of Jesus Christ was as follows: After his mother Mary was betrothed to Joseph, but before they came together, she was found with child of the Holy Spirit. Then Joseph her husband being a just man and not wanting to make her a public example, was minded to put her away secretly. But

11

while he thought about these things, behold an angel
of the Lord appeared to him in a dream saying,
'Joseph son of David, do not be afraid to take Mary
for your wife, for that which is conceived in her is
of the Holy Spirit. And she will bring forth a son,
and you shall call his name Jesus, for he will save his
people from their sins.'" Matthew 1:18-21 (NKJV).

The Bible says Joseph and Mary were *betrothed* (or
promised) to each other. Does this mean they were dating
or going out? No. In verse 18, Matthew mentions that the
two were betrothed, and Joseph is referred to as Mary's
*husband* in the next verse. Yet, in verse 20, the angel tells
Joseph not to be afraid to take to himself Mary *as his wife*.
The angel was saying, in essence, don't be afraid to go
through with the wedding ceremony.

If Joseph was called Mary's husband in one place and
later encouraged by an angel to marry her, were they
married or not? The answer is yes and no. This makes
sense once you understand Jewish betrothal and wedding
customs.

In the Jewish culture of Jesus' day, it was customary
for parents to arrange their children's marriage while the
children were still very young. By agreement, the marriage
would take place only if both the bride and groom agreed
to it when they reached marrying age.

The prospective bridegroom was expected to take the
initiative to travel from his father's house to the home
of the prospective bride. There he would negotiate the
dowry with the father of the young woman. The marriage
covenant was officially established when the bridegroom
paid the purchase price.

From that point on, the man and woman were considered to be husband and wife even though no physical union had taken place. It was also understood that once the covenant was established, the bride was set apart exclusively for the bridegroom.

Finally, a dinner was held where the bride and groom exchanged a glass of wine as confirmation that they accepted one another. The fathers of the bride and groom then pronounced a blessing upon them, symbolizing the covenant relationship between them. Once the marriage covenant is in effect, the young man returns home and builds an extension to his father's house or a house of his own.

During the period of separation between the betrothal and the marriage ceremony, the bride prepares herself for married life while the young man prepares living accommodations. At the end of the period of separation, the groom leaves his father's house (along with his best man and other men we might consider groomsmen). As we see in Matthew 25, the men conduct a torchlight procession towards the bride's house.

The bride does not know the exact hour of the bridegroom's arrival, but she and her bridesmaids (or virgins) are expecting the groom to arrive at any moment. Suddenly, they hear the sound of a *shofar* or ram's horn along with the shout, "The bridegroom is coming, the bridegroom is coming!"

Upon their arrival, the entire wedding procession follows the groom and bride with her female attendants to his father's house. The bride and groom enter the bridal chamber; the marriage is consummated, and they are considered to be married in spirit, soul, and body.

Throughout the entire betrothal period both the bride and the groom were to remain pure, just as Joseph and Mary remained pure although they were considered husband and wife.

Joseph did not understand that Mary had been made pregnant by the Holy Spirit until an angel explained what happened. According to the law, he could have ordered her stoned to death, or he could divorce her.

The Bible says that just before the angel intervened, Joesph had decided to divorce Mary privately because he did not want to humiliate her. This brings us back to the point that there was no "dating" or "going out" in the Word of God. People trusted the sovereignty of God for the choice of their future husband or wife, a process usually done through the parents and the priest. This custom continued in the New Testament.

Remember that the Word of God is the only universal absolute in the world today. Jesus Christ, who is the Word of God, said, "I am the way, the truth, and the life" (John 14:6b, NKJV). If you want truth, you have to go to the Word of God.

Does the Word of God say anything about romance? Does it say anything about guy/girl relationships? I know of three such passages in the Song of Solomon.

*"I charge you oh daughters of Jerusalem by the gazelles and by the does of the field: Do not stir up nor awaken love until it pleases." Song of Solomon 2:7* (NKJV)

*"I charge you oh daughters of Jerusalem by the gazelles and by the does of the field: Do not stir up or awaken love until it pleases." Song of Solomon 3:5* (NKJV)

*"I charge you oh daughters of Jerusalem: Do not stir up or awaken love until it pleases." Song of Solomon 8:4* (NKJV)

*"Promise me oh women of Jerusalem by the swift gazelles and the deer of the wild, do not awaken love until the time is right." Song of Solomon 8:4* (New Living Translation)

Do not get romantically involved before the time is right. Without going into too much detail about the Song of Solomon, let's consider its three key players. The first is the Shulammite, a young, unmarried woman who is very much in love with a shepherd who is her beloved.

The second is King Solomon, who has many wives and who, I believe, utilizes the daughters of Jerusalem to try to steal her love away from the shepherd. The daughters of Jerusalem appear to be women from King Solomon's court who are attempting to seduce, entice and even arouse the Shulammite into an illicit relationship with King Solomon.

The third key player is the shepherd, who has an unusual relationship with the Shulammite. In Song of Solomon 4:8 he says, "Come with me from Lebanon, *my spouse*" (emphasis mine). In verse 9 he says, "You have ravished my heart, my sister, *my spouse*; you have ravished my heart with one look of your eyes, with one link of your necklace." Verse 10 says, "How fair is your love, my sister, *my spouse!*" In verse 12 he repeats it again, "A garden enclosed is my sister, *my spouse.*" And in chapter 5 verse 1, the shepherd again says, "I have come to my garden, my sister, *my spouse.*"

When he calls her his sister, he is referring to the purity of their relationship. When the shepherd calls the Shulamite his spouse, it is possible (even though it is not stated) that they are already betrothed. It is significant that the Bible makes no reference to illicit or illegal sexual activity taking place between the Shulammite and the shepherd.

This illustrates a vital universal absolute: *Romance should wait until a person is ready for marriage.*

A great number of young people in America and Europe enter into romance and become prematurely involved in romantic relationships before they are physically, financially, and emotionally prepared for marriage.

As the Shulammite said to the women of Jerusalem on three separate occasions, "Do not awaken, or stir, or entice my love until the time is right." In other words, she was saying:

> Do not speak to me about sexual things; I am not ready now for marriage. Do not speak to me about Solomon who has many wives. I already have my beloved, the one I want to marry. Right now, we do not have a relationship that is sexual or impure. As a matter of fact, he calls me his sister, his spouse.

> I charge you women of Jerusalem: Love should be free and without restrictions. Therefore, do not try to stir up something in me now that I will not be able to stop later.

Three times the Scriptures warn us: "Do not awaken love before the time." The Bible standard for trustworthy testimony is three witnesses (see Deuteronomy 19:15, Matthew 18:16). Even the world's secular law systems tend to avoid convicting someone of a crime unless there are two or three witnesses.

Three scriptures clearly admonish us not to pursue romance until we are ready for the marriage covenant.

When we violate this warning, we essentially become a careening vehicle headed for a collision with divorce, pregnancy, sexually transmitted disease and even violence and rape.

## DISCUSSION QUESTIONS
### Questions for Parents and Young People

1. Explain how God's Word is the only universal absolute truth you can count on.

2. How does relativism affect our concept of truth?

3. When truth has been downgraded to mean what is "true for me," how does it affect our behavior and the choices that we make?

4. How many young people in your school have you noticed are going out with other young men and young women?

5. How has this affected their behavior?

6. Why do you think so many kids as young as 5, 6, and 7 are writing love notes and pursuing romantic interest with the opposite sex?

7. In Song of Solomon 2:7; 3:5, 8:4, the principle is presented that you are not to pursue or arouse love in your life until you are ready for marriage. List the "pro's and con's" of this principle from the viewpoint of modern society or from your own perspective.

## CHAPTER 3 – There's a Whole Lot Happening Inside of Me

> **Luke 2:52**
>
> "And Jesus increased in wisdom and stature, and in favor with God and men."

Jesus grew mentally, spiritually, physically, socially, and emotionally. We also grow in these five areas, and they affect our entire lives. Let's look at these areas of development that we all experience. We will especially consider how they affect our concept of love and romance. I believe that as we consider normal development in all of these areas, it will become clear that we are rushing towards premature romantic relationships.

First, we grow mentally. Philippians 2:5 tells us we are to have the mind of Christ.

"Let this mind be in you which was also in Christ Jesus," Philippians 2:5 (NKJV).

As we mature mentally, we develop in our ability to understand facts, to reason and to exercise common sense. There are basically two types of thinkers – concrete and abstract. Concrete thinkers (generally include children up to the age of 14 or 15) think in terms of what can be perceived with the five physical senses. In other words, they understand tangible things that they can see, hear, touch, taste and smell.

Since God is abstract virtually by definition, we must explain Him to concrete thinkers (such as young teenagers) by saying, for example, "God exists as God the Father, God the Son, and God the Holy Spirit. These three are one." It helps them to understand this better if we use tangible examples. For instance, "God is like an egg. There's the shell, the white of the egg, and the yoke. One egg with three different entities -- that's the way God is. What is an apple — the skin, the white part, or the pit? The answer is all three. It's hard to separate them."

Abstract thinkers (usually over the age of 14) can reason and develop an understanding of intangible things. They begin to understand, for example, the meaning of love and the concept of God. Children develop abstract thinking in school by learning reading, math, and comprehension activities.

How does concrete thinking versus abstract thinking affect a young child or a young teen when it comes to relating to the opposite sex and feelings of love and romance?

Concrete thinkers tend to view love and romance as something physical. They will be more prone to touching because they don't understand the abstract concepts of commitment, covenant, and purity. It is difficult for them to understand love beyond its physical aspects, or to grasp the notion of a lifetime commitment. Unfortunately, concrete thinkers are also more apt to become physically involved because *they would rather touch than talk.*

Several years ago in St. Petersburg, Florida, two fifteen year olds committed suicide by jumping off the Howard Franklin Bridge. The suicide notes they left behind explained their reasoning. The parents of one of the boys were moving from Florida to Ohio, and these close friends would be separated. These two *concrete thinkers* determined that "they could not live without each other" and decided to end their lives.

Concrete thinkers are poorly equipped to deal with the responsibilities of an adult relationship. God truly understood our limitations when He warned us not to awaken the concept of love before the time is right. Don't awaken passionate feelings before you have the mental capacity to help control those abstract feelings.

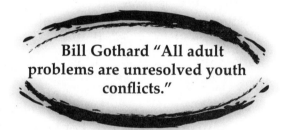

**Bill Gothard "All adult problems are unresolved youth conflicts."**

Spiritual development is the second of the five crucial areas of growth we mentioned earlier. Every Christian should have a goal of being "mighty in spirit." Paul the apostle prayed in Ephesians 3:16 "…that [God] would grant you, according to the riches of His glory, to be strengthened with might through His Spirit in the inner man," (NKJV).

When you are mighty in spirit and understanding you are prepared for life. We want our children to have favor with God and man. The spiritual must control all the other areas of life. Jesus' life as a young boy provides us with an excellent example.

*"...supposing him to have been in the company, they went a day's journey, and sought Him among their relatives and acquaintances... Then he went down with time and came to Nazareth, and was subject to them, but His mother kept all these things in hear heart. And Jesus increased in wisdom and stature, and in favor with God and men."* Luke 2: 44, 51, 52 (NKJV).

Jesus submitted to His parents even though He was sharper or more spiritually attuned than His parents. God designed young people to be under submission and obedience to their parents, even though they feel they know more or are sharper than their parents. Teenagers sometimes presume that everything is the way *they* see it. The tendency to think they know everything (when they really don't), and that they can do everything better than their elders.

The third critical area is physical development. First Corinthians 6:20 states, "For you were bought with a price, therefore, glorify God in your body and in your spirit which are God's." (NKJV). Puberty marks the stage of physical development when young people experience significant biochemical changes in their bodies. Girls experience puberty between the ages of 10 through 16. For boys, it occurs a little later between the ages of 14 through 18. Of course, this varies with each individual.

The teenage years are generally considered to be some of the most challenging years of life. This period represents a relatively short time in the average life span, but those seven years can leave an indelible mark on a person's life.

They may create wonderful memories or terrible nightmares. Teen experiences may prepare you for success, or they may set you on a course toward shipwreck and failure. Perhaps this is why the Bible refers to this period as "the difficult days."

I am convinced these difficult days refer to the passage through puberty when youngsters are developing physically and emotionally. Consider these two scriptures:

> *"Rejoice, oh young man, in your adolescence, and let your heart cheer you in the days of your full-grown youth. And walk in the ways of your heart and in the sight of your eyes, but know that for all these things God will bring you to judgment. Therefore, remove the lust that ends in sorrow and vexation from your heart and mind and put away evil from your body, for youth and the dawn of life are vanity, transitory, idle, empty and devoid of truth."* Ecclesiastes 11:9-10 (Amplified Version)

> *"Remember now your creator in the day of your youth before the difficult days come and the years draw near when you say, I have no pleasure in them."* Ecclesiastes 12:1-2 (New King James Version)

The bodies of boys and girls experiencing puberty develop at a faster rate than their emotional or social capacity. For instance, the body develops much faster than human emotions during this period. Teens often experience irritability, extreme sensitivity, loneliness, depression, and occasional giddiness. They tend to overreact in many situations because they are experiencing radical biochemical changes in their bodies. Many teens exhibit a serious lack of self control and a desire to do things their way.

An important principle to remember during these difficult years is that God is preparing adolescents for adulthood and independence. Teenagers should be encouraged to make decisions for themselves, but they should submit their decisions to their parents or their pastors. Because of the ups and downs of teenage emotions, they generally cannot trust themselves. Therefore, God places teenagers under the authority of parents, pastors, and teachers to help guide their decisions.

It is in their best interest to learn to submit to authority and not attempt to make independent decisions on major questions. They should compel themselves to submit to their authorities and not be rebellious. All major decisions should be submitted to parents and pastors. Since their bodies are growing much faster than their emotional or social development when it comes to romance and issues of love, this is not a time for teenagers to go out, go steady, or nurture romantic feelings towards the opposite sex. The diagram below illustrates why teenagers should remain under the authority and protection of their parents to avoid certain temptations.

We want our children to have favor with God and man.

All major decisions should be submitted to higher authorities, but when teenagers want to make their own decisions, it should not be interpreted as rebellion. This is God's call to parents to use every opportunity to train their children in how to be a man or woman of God.

In addition, as young people grow physically they also grow socially – they interact with others. Puberty produces powerful biochemical reactions that strongly affect teenagers. They should guard themselves during this volatile time because they may be particularly susceptible to unhealthy influences by their friends. Peer pressure is very powerful during this time because teens wrestle with an extremely strong feeling and desire to "be like everybody else."

In the area of "romance," peer pressure leads many teens to ask, "If everybody else is going out and making out, then why not me? I must be missing out on something." The Word of God admonishes us, "For we dare not compare ourselves with those who commend themselves. When they, measuring themselves by themselves and comparing themselves among themselves, are not wise." 2 Corinthians 10:12 (NKJV).

Young people want to compare themselves with others for several reasons. First of all, they have a strong desire for acceptance. It seems to me that human beings basically need three things: love, acceptance, and a sense of belonging. Love provides a sense of being wanted – a feeling of worth and significance. Acceptance creates the sense of "being needed" – a feeling of importance and value. A sense of belonging gives us an identity – a sense that we are part of something larger than ourselves.

Add to these three strong human desires the biochemical changes surging through the typical teenager, and you come up with an unusually strong desire to be accepted and be popular with other young people. The teen who wants to be accepted on this high-desire level is, therefore, easily influenced by his peers.

If Christian teenagers are not careful, they may begin to doubt the Word of God. They start to question the absolutes in their lives because "everybody else is doing it." When challenged, they often reply, "What is wrong with this, anyway?"

Compound the questioning of foundational values with the intricacies of biochemical changes and emotional fluctuations, and you begin to understand how susceptible teens can be to the influence of their peers.

If you throw in relativism (the idea that "truth is only true to me"), then most youngsters will give in to the attitude that says, "Don't knock it till you try it—how can you say it is wrong if you have never done it?"

The Word of God clearly teaches that we should learn about evil by discernment, not by experience. Romans 16:19 says, "But I want you to be wise in what is good and simple concerning evil." (NKJV). This makes it even more imperative that the pursuit of romance be delayed until one is beyond the critical teenage years.

Parents beware: Do not encourage your youngsters to enter premature romantic relationships. If you are a young person yourself, then don't give in to the popular notion that you must have a girlfriend or boyfriend. Obey God and set aside the pressures to go out with somebody. Do not awaken love before the time.

# DISCUSSION GUIDE
## Questions for Parents and Young People

1. List the characteristics of a concrete thinker, and then list those of an abstract thinker. What is your style of thinking right now?


2. How does concrete thinking affect thoughts about romance? How does abstract thinking affect thoughts about romance?


3. Explain how puberty affects the emotions and moods of a young person:


4. Since the physical body develops faster than the social and emotional development of young people, how does it affect romantic relationships?

5. Why is it imperative that teenagers submit their major decisions to their parents and pastoral authorities (especially decisions about friendships and romance)?

6. What are the three things that every human being needs? How can these needs affect a person in the area of premature romance?

7. Why is a teenager so easily influenced by his or her peers? How can this affect their outlook on romance and going out?

8. If a youth is lacking love, acceptance, and a sense of belonging, how will this affect his/her outlook on romance and the desire to go out with someone?

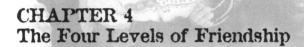

# CHAPTER 4
## The Four Levels of Friendship

Friendships directly affect romance and relationships, so it is important for us to understand the four basic levels of friendship I've found in the Word.

*The first is casual.* You might refer to a casual friend as an acquaintance because at this level you do not know the person very well. Casual friendships focus on curiosity and inquiries, and conversation tends to revolve around inquiries such as, "Where are you from?" and "Where do you live?" Scriptures to bear in mind are Proverbs 18:24, "A man who has friends must show himself to be friendly" (NKJV); and Hebrews 10:24, "And let us consider one another in order to stir up love and good works" (NKJV). Also consider Philippians 2:4, "Let each of you look out not only for his own interest, but also for the interests of others" (NKJV). You can look at casual friendships as divine appointments. God can show you something about yourself or about that person that can better your perspective on life.

*The second level is the common level of friendship.* Amos the prophet asked, "Can two walk together unless they are agreed?" Amos 3:3 (NKJV). "Interest" is the key word describing the common level of friendship. These relationships are based on common interests, activities, and concerns. There is a greater liberty to know others better, to see them more often, and to express interest in their opinions, ideas, and goals.

*The third level of friendship is a close friendship.* Proverbs 27:8 says, "Faithful are the wounds of a friend" (NKJV). The implication here is that a close friend will speak the truth in love, even if it causes you discomfort. This level of friendship is based on similar goals. You may not have total openness to share or complete confidence, but you do have the freedom to suggest alternatives, actions, and methods of achieving goals. Proverbs 18:24b says, "but there is a friend who sticks closer than a brother" (NKJV).

Important factors in a close friendship include complete honesty, openness, transparency and integrity. Trust between parties will be evident even though they may lack the confidence level that is necessary to openly speak into one another's lives. However, there will be enough openness to exchange ideas, suggestions, alternative plans, and differences of opinion.

*The fourth level of friendship is a covenant friendship.* Look at three verses about friendship:

*"Open rebuke is better than love carefully concealed."* Proverbs 27:5 (NKJV)

*"Confess your trespasses to one another and pray for one another that you may be healed."* James 5:16 (NKJV)

*"But speaking the truth in love...."* Ephesians 4:15 (NKJV)

The covenant relationship is one of intimacy, characterized by the total commitment of both parties to the development of their respective assignments, goals and desires in life. Covenant friends consider themselves confidants who may openly share the innermost secrets of the heart. They are willing to embrace extreme accountability toward one another and enjoy total freedom to correct each other in the love of God. Their relationship is characterized by a complete openness to discuss long and short-term goals.

*What does all of this have to do with romance, relationships, and going out with one another? Why do "levels of friendship" matter, and what difference does it make in my life?*

Have you ever heard married couples saying things such as, "I wish I could tell your father what is really on my mind" or "I wish I could tell your mother how I really feel"? Many couples who have been married 25 or 30 years have never reached the point where they can bare their souls to one another. Why?

The problem is they never reached the fourth level of friendship. They lack true intimacy, and I am convinced this is the number one cause of divorce in the United States and in most of the world.

The primary reason for this phenomenon is that for many couples, their early romantic relationship involved more touching than talking. That means these couples were more *physically aroused* than *spiritually connected*. I believe that they awakened love before the time.

Remember and observe this cardinal principal: *Level 4 – the covenant and intimate level of friendship – must be entered into only with a person who is going to be your future spouse and is of the opposite sex.* God never intended for two people of the opposite sex to have spiritual intercourse on this deep intimate level unless they were intended to be one another's spouse.

In our climate of rampant sexual immorality, many youngsters are experiencing raging hormones and fluctuating emotions because they go out, make out, and kiss and touch one another passionately. Physical and emotional attachment causes them to sincerely believe they are in a close relationship or a covenant relationship. In reality, they are casual friends at best.

In my opinion, most people who marry in the western world do so while in a casual or common friendship. Rarely do we see couples marry who enjoy a close or covenant relationship. The failure to experience covenant intimacy in a marriage may plant seeds of divorce and destruction that will end in ruin.

"What does this have to do with me?" you might ask. "I am only 15, and I am not even thinking about marriage."

It has everything to do with you. If you are attracted to members of the opposite sex, you should not enter into a relationship beyond Level 2 (a common relationship). Limit your relationships to the casual or common level where you can ask questions of interest and learn about one other's ideas, goals, and priorities. Above all, *do not awaken love before the time.*

If a young man's interest grows and he draws close enough to a young lady in a relationship of involvement to begin influencing her life, a progression of intimacy usually begins. Inevitably there will be increased physical attraction and arousal of sexual desires and involvement (although it may not always culminate in sexual activity). Romance and arousal will occur before the time, and this is never God's will.

In the previous chapter, I mentioned the constantly changing emotions teens experience while their bodies mature so much faster than their mental, emotional, and social capacity. If I have just described your situation, then I cannot overemphasize that the authorities in your life (such as your parents and your pastor) have the final say concerning your choice of casual or common relationships. They have your best interest in mind and must be able to stop or redirect any relationships that will not build you up. Allow them to speak into your life before you enter into an intimate covenant relationship.

Teenagers who disregard or avoid the protection of authorities on this level will face the very real danger of arousing and awakening romance *before the time*. In many if not most cases, this inevitably leads to immorality and disobedience to God.

# DISCUSSION GUIDE
## Questions for Parents and Young People

1. Define a casual friendship and give examples of questions that are exchanged at this level.

2. Define a common friendship and give the keyword to describe it.

3. Describe a close friendship and list some of the Scripture references that speak about a close friendship. To what extent should you be involved in a person's life at this level of friendship?

4. What is meant by a covenant friendship?

5. What is the primary difference between a close and a covenant friendship?


6. Examine the current friendships in your life. List their names, and write the number or level of that friendship next to the person's name.


7. Why is it important to submit friendships (especially close and covenant friendships) to your spiritual and parental authorities for their approval?


8. Why is accountability between friends so important?


9. Why is it dangerous or foolish to enter into marriage on a casual or common friendship basis?

10. How can sexual immorality (particularly when you're "going out") make people feel as if they are close or covenant friends?

# CHAPTER 5
## Squeezing God Out

In a previous chapter, we noted that we grow and develop in five different areas: spiritually, physically, mentally, emotionally, and socially. There are serious consequences in all of these areas when we hurry love before the time.

In this chapter we will discuss the spiritual consequences of rushing or wakening love before the time. The first consequence or danger is that *a young person who pursues romance prematurely is in danger of displacing Jesus as the first love in his or her life.* Jesus said, "Nevertheless, *I have this against you: you have left your first love*. Remember, therefore, from where you have fallen. Repent and do the first works or else I will come to you quickly and remove your lampstand from its place unless you repent" (Revelation 2: 4-5, NKJV, emphasis mine).

The Lord Jesus was warning the church in Ephesus about their worst sin: they no longer loved Jesus above every person, plan, possession, or thing in their lives. Jesus considered them to be in a fallen state and warned them to repent and return to their original works of service. There were serious consequences if they failed.

In other words, these individuals were backslidden; they no longer made Jesus Christ their number one priority. Having a boyfriend or girlfriend may appear innocent when romance is pursued at a very early age. It may even be *expected* at age 15 or 16. What we fail to realize is that this may easily cause young Christians to displace Jesus Christ as the first priority in their lives. This is one of the greatest sins committed by Christians of any age. We are told in Matthew 22:37, "You shall love the Lord your God with all your heart, with all your soul, and with all your mind." (NKJV).

A young person — particularly a concrete thinker — will find it almost impossible to love or claim to love someone unless they replace Jesus as the number one person in his/ her life. This command specifically says you are to love the Lord your God with all your heart. How can you do this if you prematurely give your heart away to someone else?

You are to love God with "all your soul." I have heard it said that the human soul is composed of the " mind, will, and emotions." How can we possibly love Jesus with all of our thinking, with all of our will or volition, and with all of our emotions and feelings if we are preoccupied with someone else?

"But if this is the case, how will I ever marry?" you might ask. "How do I find my future spouse if I don't go out or date around? Doesn't God expect me to look for someone?" The answer is "no."

Matthew 6:33 teaches, "Seek ye first the Kingdom of God and his righteousness, and all these things will be added to you." In essence, Jesus is automatically moved into second place when you start *looking* for a boy or girl friend (He wants to *give* you a mate, not have you *hunt* for one as if

He is powerless.) God wants you to trust His sovereignty. He wants to be the first passion and affection of your life. Go after Him with all of your heart; and, in the process, He will show you a future spouse. God usually provides clear confirmation of His blessing on the relationship — not only to both parties, but also to their respective parents and pastoral authorities.

Secondly, romance *before the right time* may rob you of your primary focus *to do your God-given assignment in life.* Have you ever wondered why you have fingerprints that are unique to you? Consider this: Our planet is home to six billion people, and not one of them has *your* fingerprints or exact DNA! Not one of them would share the blood vessel pattern you have in your eyes as determined by a retinal scan. Why? I believe these things confirm that God has given each of us a divine purpose in life. Unless you find and fulfill that purpose, you will never be happy.

*As you are faithful in your assignments to those God has placed in authority over you, and as you faithfully enable these authorities to be successful by completing your assignments to them, God will one day promote you to your own assignments and your own successes.*

You will be given assignments to complete throughout life according to 2 Timothy 1:9, which says, "[God] has saved us and called us with a Holy calling—not according to our works but according to His own purpose and grace which was given to us in Christ Jesus before the world began." Paul said in Ephesians 2:10, "For we are His workmanship, created in Christ Jesus for good works, which God prepared before hand that we should walk in them."

These good works are the purposes of God for your life. They are specific assignments or jobs for you to do that will help solve problems for others. Some of these assignments are universal. Our first major assignment is to be a son or daughter who brings glory and peace and joy to his/her parents. We also have the assignment to be students. Every job that you have is an assignment from God, so view them as direct assignments from the Lord. Jesus said in Luke 16:11, "Therefore, if you have not been faithful in what is another man's, who will give you what is your own?"

This is an important principle: *As you are faithful in your assignments to those God has placed in authority over you, and as you faithfully enable these authorities to be successful by completing your assignments to them, God will one day promote you to your own assignments and your own successes.*

Hurrying romance ahead of God's timing threatens your primary focus to complete your God given assignments in life. It may blind you and totally refocus the direction of your life away from God's perfect will. Set your focus during the teenage years on assignment to excel in school and youth church and to be an excellent son or daughter.

God has a perfect focus for you. When you spend your time pursuing romance prematurely you may rob yourself of your focus. Can you imagine the regret you would feel if God gave you a divine dream for your life, an incredible vision of what you have always wanted to do—but you prematurely sapped the strength of that dream through a premature involvement in a romantic relationship God never asked you to enter into?

Millions of young people will spend their lives chasing dreams that will never be fulfilled because they developed a pattern of awakening love before the time. How many will fall into the deception and distraction of focusing their time, money, energy, emotions and strength trying to make *another person* happy instead of pleasing Jesus?

Jesus said in the parable of the sower, "Now the ones that fell among the thorns are those who when they have heard go out and our choked with the cares, riches, and pleasures of life and bring no fruit to maturity" (Luke 8:14, NKJV). The Lord explained that when the seed of God's Word is preached some people quickly receive the Word and try to bear the fruit of Christianity—but their fruit is choked by the cares, riches, and pleasures of life. I call them "The 3 P's – Pain, Possessions, and Pleasures."

The cares of life are the pains we experience. Everyone gets hurt, and pain can choke the Word of God out of your life and prevent you from bearing fruit. Premature romance can bring much pain. Giving too much attention to possessions (buying gifts, bestowing lavish presents in premature romance) can choke the fruit of the Spirit out of your life.

What are the "pleasures of life"? One of the best examples may be the choice of young people who feel they have to obtain pleasure from a boy or girl friend instead of from their relationship with the Lord Jesus Christ. They awaken love before the time and can't handle it emotionally. They essentially choke and squeeze Jesus out of their lives when their main concern becomes pleasure. They tend to focus more on feeling good and pleasing the other person in their romantic relationship than on pleasing Jesus.

# DISCUSSION GUIDE
## Questions for Parents and Young People

1. How can a dating or "going out" relationship replace Jesus as the first love in a young person's heart?

2. What are some of your assignments in life right now, and what kind of problems are you solving for your parents, teachers, or employer?

3. Have you discovered your purpose in life? Explain why God put you, in particular, on this planet? (Whatever bothers you or moves you with compassion could be a hint as to your eternal purpose in God.)

4. Are you successful in your relationships with those in authority over you?

5. Are you fulfilling your assignments with excellence and a good attitude?

6. How might a premature romantic relationship affect your God-given assignments in life?

# CHAPTER 6
# I think I'm in Love, I think I'm in Love

We have discussed the spiritual effects of hurrying romance, now we must examine the emotional effects of awakening love before the time.

The first effect of hurrying romance is that *it often leads to overwhelming feelings of love and premature sex*. As we noted earlier, Jesus said, "Nevertheless, I have this against you, that you have left your first love" (Revelation 2:4, NKJV). Jesus is saying, "I want to be number one in your life."

In my mind's eye, I see a picture of Jesus looking at the church in the U.S.A. Tears are running down His cheeks as He considers what so many call the hope of America— the young people—so consumed with pleasure seeking through boyfriends and girlfriends. (They spend hours together, then go home and spend more time with each other on the phone or on the Internet.)

In most cases, it is easy to determine who is the focus of your affections: with whom do you spend the most time? Who occupies your thoughts throughout the typical twenty-four-hour period? How can we say we love Jesus when we can't wait to get out of church so we can spend time with a boy or girl friend? We break the heart of God with this type of behavior.

Many young people feel and believe they love someone when it is nothing more than the emotional consequence of hurrying love. Yet, there is another more dangerous emotional consequence of awakening love before the time. I call it "the urge to merge," the excitement and desire to explore sexual feelings outside of the marriage covenant.

The world teaches – *If you love me, you'll let me.* Teenagers should not be under that kind of pressure. God gave us sexual feelings along with the capacity and urge for sex, but only within the marriage covenant between a husband and wife. God never meant for us to awaken the passion of love before entering into marriage.

If you recall the illustration of the car crash in chapter 1, love and romance are similar to that crash in that sex was never meant to be started if you have to stop before you go all the way. It may cause you to do something that as a Christian you will regret.

Many young men and women find themselves in passionate embraces and long kisses (and under deep conviction), being forced to "put on the brakes" before doing something that is unscriptural and ungodly.

If the "car of sexual desire were still in the garage," you wouldn't have to say no or put on the brakes. There is a good reason that the Word of God says "Do not awaken love before the time." By God's design, once a married couple engages in foreplay, they will consummate that time with the gift of sex. When two unmarried people arouse passion and sense the conviction of the Holy Spirit that they are fornicating, they may attempt to stop. Unfortunately, they will find it increasingly difficult to put on the brakes each time because the urge to have sex grows stronger and stronger.

*The interpretation of sexual feelings such as lust and arousal as true intimacy and love* is another serious consequence of awakening love before the time. Youngsters may be deceived into believing that they are in the fourth level or covenant friendship (where there is intimacy of the spirit and the soul) when actually there is only physical intimacy. They begin to talk about marriage prematurely and sow seeds of divorce that may erode or break up their future marriage if indeed they marry.

The premature arousal of romantic feelings often has another serious emotional consequence. As a young person begins to "fall in love" with someone prematurely, *they begin to erode relationships with their parents, pastors, fellow Christians and even other friends.* The closer together they come, the more they exclude and withdraw from other people. Romantically involved teens who work often begin to lose interest in their jobs. More importantly, their relationships with God and the authorities in their lives suffer and grow distant.

If you compound these problems with the destructive pattern of *multiple* involvements—going out, breaking up, going out and breaking up in four or five relationships—then you have a young heart that has been scarred emotionally by broken relationships. Young people seem to change boyfriends and girlfriends so often that by the time they marry, they have become efficient in the art of breaking up and withdrawing. I have to believe this plants seeds for divorce later on.

The rise of resentment and bitterness in the heart is yet another consequence of going out and breaking up repeatedly. Sometimes these embittered young men and women even feel  anger towards God and other people.

Depression, sparked by feelings of guilt, resentment and of "being used" may even lead to suicide in extreme cases. I've heard the U.S. has the highest level of teen suicides in the world. Unfortunately, suicide can be the ultimate emotional consequence of the premature arousal of love and romance.

# DISCUSSION GUIDE
## Questions for Parents and Young People

1.  How can going out or dating someone lead to premature feelings of love and sexual experimentation?

2.  What are some of the signs that a boyfriend/girlfriend relationship is moving towards the physical?

3.  What is the danger of interpreting lust as love?

4.  What are the dangers of a couple drawing close to each other at the expense of withdrawing from other major relationships in their lives?

5. Explain why multiple breakups with boyfriends/ girlfriends may lead to emotional scars in a young person's life?

6. Explain how feelings of resentment, anger, and even suicide develop in someone who often has broken up intimate relationships?

7. Are you seeing or going out with someone now? (Do you see the warning signs of awakening love before the time?)

8. Parents, do you know whether or not your child is currently involved in a relationship?

## CHAPTER 7
## If You Love Me,
## You'll Let Me

Millions of young people in America and Europe today are playing a form of "Russian Roulette" with their bodies and their emotions. God created

> **Deuteronomy 19:15**
>
> One witness shall not rise against a man concerning any iniquity or any sin that he commits. By the mouth of two or three witnesses the matter shall be established."

the "engine of desire" to fire up and burn for a lifetime of marital romance and fulfillment. He never intended for romance to have "brakes" on it.

Do you remember the illustration in chapter 1 concerning the car and the collision? Romance and sexuality were never intended to be a process that would start and stop repeatedly. God intended for sexuality to be experienced only between a husband and wife, where it would be allowed to develop *without interruption*. Today, we have a system in our society called "romance," "going steady" or "going out" in which young people "make out" or touch one another intimately. This often culminates in either sexual intercourse or deception. Even Christians who should know better actually believe they can touch, pet, make-out, and passionately kiss without problems. They tell themselves that it is not sin "as long as we do not proceed to physical intercourse." What a deception! That is absolutely against the Word of God.

Let's look at the physical consequences of awakening and hurrying love and romance before the time.

First of all, it prematurely awakens the curiosity of young people towards sex. Sex is a wonderful thing. It is a gift from God that should be explored only within the confines of the marriage covenant. Unnatural arousal occurs when six- and seven-year-olds begin to write love notes and to stir up affections that God intended to occur many years later.

Second, when young people rush into romance, it may lead to flirting and then to promiscuity. Awakening romance before the time instills the notion in young ladies that the prettier and sexier they look, the greater their chances to attract young men. The danger, of course, is that it will engender *lust* in young men, and it will defraud them. "Defrauding" is a biblical term referring to the seduction or sexual corruption of another person (to take advantage of another person). Young women should never use their bodies to "be sexy" so they can sexually arouse young men. 1 Thessalonians 4:3-7 (NKJV) states:

> "For this is the will of God, your sanctification: that you should abstain from sexual immorality; that each of you should know how to possess his own vessel in sanctification and honor, not in passion of lust, like the Gentiles, who do not know God; that no one should take advantage and defraud his brother in this manner, because the Lord is the avenger of all such, as we also forewarned you and testified. For God did not call us to uncleanness, but to holiness."

Third, rushing into romance may lead a couple into intimate touching, petting (heavy touching for sexual arousal), and fornication. We read in 1 Corinthians 7:1 (NKJV), "Now concerning the things of which you wrote to me, it is good for a man not to *touch* a woman" (emphasis mine). The word touch is the same word that Jesus used when Mary Magdalene thought he was the gardener and he told her, "Do not touch me" or "do not cling to me" (see John 20:17). The context of 1 Corinthians 7:1, which says, "It is good for a man not to touch a woman," refers to touching in an inordinate or inappropriate manner (or what young people would call "turning her on").

The Scriptures teach that the only time a man and a woman can touch each other in an arousing way is within the marriage covenant. One of the greatest deceptions in the body of Christ today may be the notion that young people can make out, kiss passionately, and touch each other in various parts of the body without sin. They believe that they have not fornicated as long as they don't "go all the way" (have sexual intercourse). That is one of the biggest lies of the devil. Heavy petting is fornication. The word, fornication, comes from the Greek root word, porneia, from which we get the word pornography. It refers to sex outside of the marriage covenant; and that includes any sexual acts that arouse feelings of lust between two unmarried people.

The devil deceives youngsters all over the world into thinking that as long as the sexual act was not consummated everything is fine. This is not so. If a young couple makes out heavily and then manages to stop before they go "all the way," they should not think that they have not fornicated – they have.

Young people throughout the U.S. — especially in junior high schools — are engaging in inordinate sexual practices but stop short of consummating "coitus" or the final sexual act.

The fourth physical consequence of hurrying romance is obvious: It often leads youngsters into total sexual activity. The increase of sexually transmitted diseases and unwanted pregnancies indicates the problem of fornication is growing. While many say, "Everybody's doing it," the Word of God is clear – we are not to fornicate. Hebrews 13:4 says, "Marriage is honorable among all and the bed undefiled, but fornicators and adulterers God will judge." (NKJV). Galatians 5:19 lists fornication as one of the works of the flesh, and verse 21 states, "Those who practice such things will not inherit the Kingdom of God." (NKJV).

Self-gratification is another physical consequence that results when love and romantic feelings are aroused before the time. The simplest definition for self-gratification or masturbation is "to touch or stimulate oneself to feel good sexually." God never intended for us to engage in such self-pleasure because He had *marriage* in mind. Many doctors and psychologists today will say this is normal behavior, but it is not. It is sin. The Bible calls it fornication. We must remember that it is impossible to engage in this type of behavior without having someone in mind. Do not let anyone tell you that masturbation is normal and acceptable behavior. It may well lead to fornication and sexual problems after marriage.

Finally, another physical consequence of arousing and hurrying love and romance is that it may lead to overt rebellion against authority. One of the clearest signs that a person is engaging in sexual immorality or moral impurity is their increased resistance to authority. In 2 Peter 2:10 (NKJV), the apostle Peter says, "And especially those who walk according to the flesh in the lust of uncleanness and despise authority, they are presumptuous, self willed, they are not afraid to speak evil of dignitaries." When I see persistent rebellion in someone, I usually suspect lust. In Jude 8 (NKJV), we read, "Likewise also these dreamers defile the flesh, reject authority and speak evil of dignitaries."

The problem is that sexual immorality causes young people to compromise or distort the Word of God to justify their impurity. God did not design us to live with guilt and conviction. Therefore, some will either cast doubt on the Word of God or seek to justify their own actions to rid themselves of guilt. The Bible indicates that this will happen in the last days. 2 Timothy 3:1-4 (NKJV) says:

> But know this, that in the last days perilous times will come: For men will be lovers of themselves, lovers of money, boasters, proud, blasphemers, disobedient to parents, unthankful, unholy, unloving, unforgiving, slanderers, without self-control, brutal, despisers of good, traitors, headstrong, haughty, lovers of pleasure rather than lovers of God.

Paul goes on to say in 2 Timothy 4:3-4 (NKJV), "For the time will come when they will not endure sound doctrine, but according to their own desires, because they have itching ears, they will heap up for themselves teachers; and they will turn their ears away from the truth, and be turned aside to fables."

It will be very popular to fornicate in the last days. It will be common for young people to go out with many different guys and girls *before* marriage (if marriage even enters into the picture). It will also be very popular — even for church people — to justify their own immorality by practicing relativism. They will say, "I just don't see it that way. I don't agree with it. That's just not true to me. I disagree. I'm going to a church where I don't feel any conviction for my actions." This is what it means to "heap to themselves teachers because they have itching ears."

# DISCUSSION GUIDE
## Questions for Parents and Young People

1. What are some of the signs of being flirtatious or promiscuous?

2. Why are "touching, making out, and heavy petting" the same as fornication?

3. Will a person who continually practices fornication inherit the kingdom of God? (see Galatians 5:19-21)

4. Why would a fornicator compromise the Word of God, and how would he or she do it?


5. How are lust and immorality associated with rebellion to authority?

# CHAPTER 8
## You're Going Out With My Ex

There are serious social consequences to hurrying and arousing love and romance before the time. For one thing, it leads to *competition* for girlfriends and boyfriends. This is the number one cause of splits in church youth groups. Philippians 2:3-4 says (NKJV), "Let nothing be done for selfish ambition or conceit, but in lowliness of mind, let each esteem others better than himself. Let each of you look out not only for his own interest, but also for the interest of others."

Many youth groups struggle with fierce competition among guys and girls for the attention of members of the opposite sex. This leads to jealousy, wrath, and strife. 2 Corinthians 12:20 (NKJV) says, "For I fear lest, when I come, I shall not find you such as I wish, and that I shall be found by you such as you do not wish; lest there be contentions, jealousies, outbursts of wrath, selfish ambitions, backbitings, whisperings, conceits, tumults." It seems that youth pastors and parents constantly deal with these problems at church and at home. This often occurs, for example, when a young man goes out with a girl who previously dated a friend of his in the same youth group.

I wonder how many fights breakout in middle and high schools because of romantic triangles, jealousies and wrath? This type of behavior can quickly turn into hatred and even physical violence.

In contrast, Ephesians 4:32 (NKJV) says, "Be kind to one another, tenderhearted, forgiving one another just as God in Christ forgave you." You cannot have hatred in your heart and love God. This hatred can be caused by hurrying love before the time.

Youngsters feel a tremendous social peer pressure to "go out," and are made to feel as if something is wrong with them if they are not dating. Many are teased mercilessly if they don't have a date for the prom, for the school dance, or even if they have not dated for a while. Some are even accused of being gay or homosexual. Peer pressure exerts a tremendous force on youths to be "just like everybody else" and engage in sexual activities because "everybody is doing it." In the process, many Christian young people end up compromising their love for Jesus and the Word of God.

> There has always been a relationship between people who walk in lust and despise authority. One of the main reasons is that they are presumptuous – they assume they are right and everybody else is wrong.

Let us reconsider the issue of "rebellion against authority." By definition the sexually immoral and the morally impure are resistant to authority. Otherwise, they would be sexually moral and morally pure. We learned in 2 Peter 2:10 (NKJV), "...those who walk according to the flesh in the lust of uncleanness and despise authority, they are presumptuous and self-willed, they are not afraid to speak evil of dignitaries." According to the Bible, there is a clear link between walking in lust and despising authority. One of the main reasons for this is that people who do these things are presumptuous – they assume they are right and everybody else is wrong. They are self-willed and primarily concerned with "me, myself and I." Therefore, they have no respect for authorities, whether parental, school, civil, or otherwise.

Jude 1:8 (NKJV), says, "Likewise also these dreamers defile the flesh, reject authority, and speak evil of dignitaries." It has been my experience as a pastor that when youngsters start getting bad grades, talking back to their parents, cutting classes, and breaking curfew; usually there is reason to suspect sexual immorality and impurity.

## DISCUSSION GUIDE
### Questions for Parents and Young People

1. How can the quest for going out cause competition among friends?


2. What negative consequences result from "girlfriend/boyfriend" and "going out" relationships?


3. How does sexual immorality or moral impurity make young people rebellious towards those in authority in the home, the church, the school, and elsewhere?

4. List the names of at least three "boyfriend/girlfriend" and "going out" relationships among your friends (list first names only):

5. Are they drawing closer to the Lord Jesus Christ? Have you observed greater obedience on their part to God's Word and to those in authority?

6. Are you going out with someone right now? Do you see any of these characteristics in your life?

# CHAPTER 9
## Can't Get Her Out of My Mind

What are some of the mental consequences of awakening and hurrying love and romance before the time? Perhaps the first consequence is described in Proverbs 23:7 (NKJV): "For as he thinks in his heart, so is he." According to the Bible, a young man who constantly thinks about a young woman may be consumed with her . . . "so is he." In other words, she will constantly occupy his thoughts.

The Word of the Lord calls this *idolatry*. It means "to exalt a person, place, or thing above God." Here is a very important principal in life: *Whatever preoccupies your thinking preoccupies your focus and will determine your direction in life. Your direction, in turn, will determine your decisions; and your decisions will determine your destiny.* Idolatry is sin. It led Israel into sin and rebellion against God and eventually caused them to be scattered by God! In Galatians 5, idolatry is listed as one of the works of the flesh, and Paul said those who practice these things will not inherit the kingdom of God.

Another mental consequence of arousing and hurrying love and romance is *spiritual blindness*. Ephesians 4:17-18 (NKJV) says:

This I say, therefore, and testify in the Lord, that

you should no longer walk as the rest of the Gentiles walk, in the futility of their mind, having their understanding darkened, being alienated from the life of God, because of the ignorance that is in them, because of the blindness of their heart.

What does Paul mean by "as the rest of the gentiles walk"? More plainly, how is it that so many non-Christian young people seem to be involved in a lifestyle of arousing love and romance as early as grade school?

In American society, and indeed the Western world, we have *trained* our children to arouse love before the time. We find it "cute" when third graders write love notes, and fourth grade boys make telephone calls to girls at their homes after school. Many parents consider this to be normal behavior. No, this is emphatically unscriptural behavior.

Even those of us in the church have been brainwashed and deceived into thinking that our young people must behave like the rest of society. Born-again

**Matthew 22:37**
"Jesus said to him, "'You shall love the Lord your God with all your heart, with all your soul, and with all your mind.'"
(NKJV)

young people who are filled with God's Spirit have a new mind, a new understanding and a new nature. They do not have to behave according to the world's standards. Once they were blind, but now they see (see John 9:25). However, if young people continue to arouse love and romance before the time, I believe they are walking in darkness and "in the futility of their minds." Their entire mental capacity will be affected in all they try to do.

A further mental consequence of arousing and hurrying romance before the time is that young people will be *exposed to idolatry*. In 1 Samuel 15:23, God likens idolatry to stubbornness—"For rebellion is as the sin of witchcraft, and stubbornness is as iniquity and idolatry." (NKJV).

How is stubbornness related to idolatry? If idolatry is exalting a person, place, or thing above God, then stubbornness is exalting our opinion above the Word of God. For example, stubbornness describes the actions of a young person who says, "I don't see it that way," or "I don't agree with that scripture—it's not true to me. It means nothing to me." Rebellion is resisting the authority of one's parents' saying, "I don't need to listen to you. I'm old enough to have my own opinions." A person who is mentally consumed by an idolatrous relationship with another person (because love has been awakened before the time) can no longer love the Lord with all of his or her heart, soul, and mind (see Matthew 22:37).

Finally, another mental consequence of arousing and hurrying love before the time is what we learned in Matthew 12:34b (NKJV): *"For out of the abundance of the heart the mouth speaks"*. In other words, what is inside shows up outside. If a young man is mentally consumed with a love and passion for his girlfriend, he will constantly speak about her. These three things reveal where your priorities are: (1) your conversation; (2) how you spend your money; and (3) how you occupy your time. If a young man prematurely (long before marriage) speaks about his girlfriend constantly, if he spends most of his time with her, and if he spends a lot of his money on her; then his god is his girlfriend and not Jesus Christ. I want to encourage you: Let your mind be transformed by the power of the Spirit of God and do not allow the world to conform you to its ways (see Romans 12:1-2).

# DISCUSSION GUIDE
## Questions for Parents and Young People

1. How can your thoughts determine the direction of your life?

2. What is idolatry?

3. How is idolatry related to stubbornness?

4. What three things determine your priorities?

5. Honestly list the things that constantly preoccupy your mind.

# CHAPTER 10
## Divorce Rehearsal

The Word of God says in Psalms 11:3 (NKJV), "If the foundations are destroyed, what can the righteous do?" The current divorce rate in the U.S.A. is staggering. A statistic from "The Americans for Divorce Reform" estimates that 40 to 50 percent of marriages will end in divorce if current trends continue. On December 21, 1999, the Barna Research Group concluded in a survey that eleven percent of the adult population is currently divorced. Twenty-five percent of adults have had at least one divorce during their lifetime. And, the divorce rate among conservative Christians was much higher than other faith groups.

The report goes on to say, "Overall, 33 percent of all born again individuals who have been married have gone through a divorce—which is statistically identical to the 34 percent incidence among non born-again adults. The fastest growing marital status category is divorced persons."

According to Arlene Saluter in "Marital Status and Living Arrangements: March 1994," a publication of the U.S. Bureau of Census, "While there are many factors that contribute to the staggering divorce rate, *the highest in the Western world*, I believe the American dating system is the primary culprit for this" [emphasis mine]. Beth Baily writes in her book, *From Front Porch to Back Seat: Courtship in Twentieth Century America:*

> A century ago, the practice of a suitor calling on a young woman at her home was common place. Dating wasn't born until the advent of the automobile which allowed teenaged boys to take teenaged girls away from their families for the evening and gradually eroded the parent's authority."

America and the rest of the world used to practice "courtship" before the arrival of the automobile. Some places even practiced betrothal as it is pictured in the Word of God. We quoted Psalms ll:3 earlier: "If the foundations are destroyed, what can the righteous do?" Jesus described the importance of foundations in Matthew 7:24-27 (NKJV):

> Therefore whoever hears these sayings of Mine, and does them, I will liken him to a wise man who built his house on the rock: and the rain descended, the floods came, and the winds blew and beat on that house; and it did not fall, for it was founded on the rock. But everyone who hears these sayings of Mine, and does not do them, will be like a foolish man who built his house on the sand: and the rain descended, the floods came, and the winds blew and beat on that house; and it fell. And great was its fall.

Jesus expects you and I to build our lives upon the Word of God. That means you build your life on an eternal value system and not a temporal one. Marriage requires the same stable foundation for success. It is certain that you will experience problems in marriage. The "rains and floods and winds" in Jesus' teaching compare to the crises and temptations that every marriage must endure. If your marriage is not built upon the principles and eternal foundations of God's Word, then it stands little chance of survival.

The American dating or going-out system reminds me of the man who built his house upon the sand. His value system was worldly and temporary. Those who approach marriage with a foundation of dating or going out are trying to build on an unstable and very *new* so-called foundation. Dating only became popular over the last 100 years. It is no wonder today that the majority of marriages choose divorce when the rains of temptation come, along with floods of crises and wind-driven problems.

Why is the failure rate so high? It is because most modern marriages in the U.S. were built upon the weak foundation initiated years earlier by the fantasy of an American dating system.

*What are some of the fallacies and dangers of dating or going out?*

Fallacy number one says, *"Dating helps you to find a marriage partner."* No, it helps you create a marriage failure. You might ask, "If I don't go out with anybody, how am I ever going to find my future spouse?" The answer is simple: You should run after God. Pursue the Lord and trust Him for the rest. Matthew 6:33 (NKJV) says, "… seek first the kingdom of God and His righteousness, and all these things shall be added to you." As you seek after God, He will eventually lead you to your future husband or wife. God is the one who rewards and blesses.

Fallacy number two claims: *"Dating or going out will help you avoid loneliness."* On the contrary, no young man or

woman could ever fill the void in your life. God intended
for you to be secure in Him and Him alone. In His
sovereignty, He will choose a partner for your life.

Fallacy number three says: *"Dating can help meet certain
needs in a person's life and also be very enjoyable."* In reality,
God intends to meet our needs through the healthy process
of friendships or marriage. God uses social relationships to
help build and edify us. On a permanent level, He provides
a marriage partner to meet our need for emotional security.

As far as having fun and feeling good, *broken relationships*
have caused many to experience incredible pain, rejection,
resentment, and wounds of the heart. In his excellent book,
*A Match Made in Heaven,* Rev. Richard Crisco, President of
the Brownsville Revival School of Ministry, outlines some
of the dangers and fallacies of dating.

One of them is that dating helps us to get to know the
other person. The problem is that "the person you take
out on a date" is not the real person because they put on
their best face and behavior. You see them at their best. By
the time you get to know the real person, you are already
emotionally attached.

Secondly, there is the delusion that dating a lot of people
is healthy and prepares you for marriage. God designed
you to be a one-woman man or a one-man woman.
However, we teach our youth that it is healthy to give
themselves to one another emotionally in a series of dating
relationships before marriage. If you date many people,
you must also break-up with many people. This sad cycle
produces wounded hearts that will eventually develop
emotional calluses and a defense against the depths of
grief.

The American dating system leads you to make and break a series of intimate relationships by which you give away your heart to many people. You stick to Person A for a while then suddenly you break up, leaving an irreplaceable piece of your heart with that person. You then try to initiate another relationship and stick to Person B for a while. Then you break up and a piece of your heart goes with that person (and a part of their heart remains with you). By the time you get to the fourth, fifth, or sixth relationship, and finally marry your spouse, you may find that it is much more difficult to give yourself away.

If you stick and "un-stick" a piece of duct tape over and over again, it quickly becomes useless because it loses its ability to stick to anything anymore. If you stick and "unstick" the affections of your heart to a crowd of people in the dating game, then one day you may discover that you can't stick or adhere to anyone else anymore.

We find we are more skeptical and less trusting of others because of the wounds and calluses suffered in previous relationships. These things prevent us from getting close to the latest "love interest." I call this "duct tape relationships."

Reverend Crisco also points out that dating promotes romance, *not* genuine love. A good definition of romance is "to woo and to attract another person by presenting and even exaggerating the best side of yourself while hiding and not showing the real you." Indeed, one of the synonyms for romance is the word "falsehood." It's interesting that the word romance doesn't even appear in the Bible, but the word love appears 551 times.

As a pastor, I have observed the following causes of divorce between married couples:

1. the lack of parental and pastoral blessing;
2. premarital defrauding and fornication;
3. emotional baggage from previous relationships;
4. a lack of intimacy and friendship between husband and wife;
5. a break down in communication;
6. financial bondage;
7. sexual dysfunction;
8. infidelity;
9. abuse (physical, chemical, emotional, or alcohol-related); and
10. a controlling attitude.

I strongly believe that the root causes of divorce can be found very early in the lives of the husband and wife. Very often I find that they began to awaken love and romance before the time. They aroused an early interest in the opposite sex and entered into the practice of dating. Along the way they gathered emotional baggage and suffered scars, and the cycle grew worse because their "relational duct tape" had lost its ability to stick. If they entered marriage without a blessing from their natural foundation—their parents—then they filled a prescription for disaster and divorce.

I have noticed a very interesting phenomenon occurring among college students and graduates recently. It seems that many young women are now reluctant to date. They prefer other alternatives to dating (and some of them are even worse).

A recent survey by the Independent Woman's Forum noted:

> Many college women prefer so-called hook-ups to dating. Hook-ups are defined as encounters ranging from kissing to sexual intercourse where both participants expect nothing afterwards. More than a third, 39 percent of respondents, describe themselves as virgins and 40 percent say they had hook-ups. Ten percent of college women responding to the poll said that they had hooked up more than six times. According to the survey, the traditional dating culture is less prevalent. Women said they are rarely asked out on dates and instead experience romantic encounters during informal gatherings of male and female friends referred to as hanging out. The poll said 91 percent of college women reported what was described as a rampant hook-up culture on their campuses. There's this group think mentality in which people go out in packs because it's the comfortable thing to do."

Love is a wonderful experience under the sovereignty of God. What once used to be the experience of thousands throughout the world—the experience of courtship and betrothal—has now deteriorated to dating, going out, and most recently, "hooking up." We must return to biblical standards. We must not encourage the awakening of love and arousing of romance in our young people before they're ready for marriage.

# DISCUSSION GUIDE
## Questions for Parents and Young People

1. In your opinion, what are the major reasons for divorce in the United States and the Western world today?

2. How long has the system of dating or going out been around?

3. Why do you think Christians trust God for salvation, but prefer to trust their own ability to choose marriage partners by dating around?

4. What are some of the fallacies and dangers of dating and going out?

5. List the "pros and cons" of dating or going out:

6. How can dating or going out prepare a young person for divorce instead of marriage?

7. If a sixteen year old is currently going out with someone and has no intention of marrying for at least five years, what is the primary reason for going out?

8. Describe the ways such a couple can fall into compromise and sin.

# CHAPTER 11
## You Are Being Brainwashed

The story of the Trojan horse is extremely relevant to the premature hurrying of love and romance. According to legend, the ancient Greeks besieged a city called Troy for ten years. Despite their best efforts, the Greeks could not capture the city because it was protected by high stone walls. Finally, the leader of the Greeks devised a daring plan to deceive the Trojans. He ordered his troops to build a huge wooden horse as a supposed "gift" to the Trojans honoring their defeat of the Greeks. Unknown to the Trojans, The Greeks had hidden a small group of elite soldiers inside the horse. Their mission was to wait in hiding for the opportune moment to exit the horse and open the gates of the city.

The Greek navy sailed beyond the view to the Trojan observers and the Greek army feigned a retreat, and the people of Troy began rejoicing. When they saw the huge wooden horse in front of the gates of the city, they were fooled into thinking that the Greeks had left them a gift as a token of their bravery. The people of Troy were lulled into a false sense of security and premature celebration. During the festive celebration, they cried for the Trojan horse to be pulled into the city square inside the gates of the city. One of the priests named Laocoon warned the people that this was a ruse and a deceptive trick on the part of the Greeks, saying, "Do not pull the horse within the gates of the city, but guard it and remain vigilant."

However, no one listened because everyone was in a mood for festivity and celebration. Very late in the night after the population was in stupor from alcohol or asleep, the Greek soldiers let themselves down from the belly of the wooden horse. They quickly overcame the remaining guards and opened the gates to the city. The Greek army then rushed through the gates, killed most of the population and burned the city.

What does this have to do with love and romance and the choosing of a future spouse? Courtship has been society's vehicle of choice since the earliest times in Europe and North America for choosing a husband or wife. Young people were expected to be friends in a wholesome relationship that included very little if any physical contact.

If a friendship evolved from a platonic relationship into one of mutual attraction, the young man would—after discussing it with the young lady—speak to his family. If his family approved, he would meet with the young lady's father to ask for her hand in marriage.

Upon receiving the approval and blessing of the father, the couple would begin the courtship process. At this point, he would spend most of his time in his fiancee's house getting to know the family. The couple would also spend a good deal of time in the home of the prospective groom. (After all, the best way to get to know your future spouse is to know his or her family.)

It was unheard of for a couple to spend time alone under the courtship system. Protocol demanded that a couple be accompanied by chaperones if they met outside the home.

In the meantime, the young man diligently saved his money and prepared to establish their future home. During this time in America, divorce was rare, and it was considered taboo. The term "single parent" was rarely heard during the early 1600's to 1900, and it was most unusual to hear of children being born out of wedlock as it was considered extremely immoral.

The sure foundation of the Word of God, built with the stones of morality and integrity, was very strong in America in those days, much like the high stone walls of Troy. Then Satan brought in a Trojan horse, a great deception designed to erode America's sense of morality and penetrate the biblical foundation of the courtship process.

Several technological inventions appeared in the late 1800's that inadvertently but directly affected the courtship process. Thomas Edison invented the phonograph in 1877 and, for the first time, the sound of the big dance bands was brought into homes. The phonograph was light and inexpensive, and dancing became more popular than ever. Dancing brought closeness and intimacy into the homes of Americans, and it increased intimate touching and arousal between young couples.

After many failures, Thomas Edison also succeeded in inventing the electric incandescent light—the light bulb—in late October of 1879. Now, couples could stay out later. They were left alone on visits in the front porch as chaperones, one by one, had to retire because of their sleepiness.

Motion pictures came on the scene in 1889, bringing still pictures to life. The motion picture industry developed quickly and movie theaters sprang up all over the U.S.

Couples began going to movies that featured romantic adventure as a form of entertainment. Young couples could now see, hear and almost feel the touch of the characters on the big screen. For the first time, couples could be defrauded into seeing romantic, artificial acts of love. It was a natural progression for people to fantasize in their minds those same actions between themselves.

The light bulb made "night life" possible. The streets were lit, phonographs and movie theaters were available, and night life became a reality in the U.S. and most of Europe. This introduced the opportunity for artificial romance, a false sense of love, and the eradication of the social institution known as courtship. Truly, Satan's Trojan horse began to release its Greek soldiers in the form of immorality and deception.

Couples no longer followed the established practice of submitting the relationship to their parents and pastors. For the very first time, couples began to decide for themselves whom they would marry. They could now go out, date, and have fun without consideration of commitment to marriage.

This erosion of courtship and the rise of immorality triggered a downward spiral that has brought America to be in its present state of moral decadence with high divorce rates and eroded family values. Early in its history, the motion picture industry had a censor board to insure moral standards. This board of individuals regulated the moral fiber and content of all movies. In the 1950's and early 1960's, however, a movement arose to remove the censorship board from the motion picture industry.

By the early 1960's, movies were no longer censored and sexually explicit motion pictures were permitted in movie theaters. This resulted in an increased level of illicit romance, artificial love, and premature arousal of romance in America's young people and throughout the western world.

In addition to this, the debut of television brought the questionable values of the motion picture industry right into the homes of Americans. By the early 1950's, televisions began to appear in American homes by the thousands, and then by the millions.

Just as the phonograph eliminated the need for a live band, television eliminated the need for frequent trips to the movie theater, and its short programming successfully mesmerized and entertained millions. Courtship further declined because couples began to spend many hours watching television programs. Many of these programs were filled with romantic illusion the eroded morality and defrauded American couples even more.

Television still has an unusually strong effect in the emotional and social lives of Americans. Television also brought the values and images of motion pictures, dance bands, pop music, and the latest dance craze right into America's living rooms.

Who can forget Dick Clark's "American Bandstand," the pop music sensation watched by millions for decades? American youths began to experiment with sensual twists and gyrations of the body showing the latest "cool" moves. Young American couples learned how to squeeze one another and slow dance in a way that encouraged sexual arousal; they were defrauded with the illusion that they must be falling in love.

Americans were inadvertently brainwashed on a mass level. They began to believe the myth that love is a *personal* selection process rather than a *family* selection process. As premature love and romance became the acceptable norm; then youngsters were expected to engage repeatedly in dating, going steady, and going out with different partners before independently (without benefit of parental or pastoral counsel) choosing the "one" to marry. This was in complete violation of the established culture (and the *successful* methods) honored for centuries in Europe and the U.S., and rooted in biblical standards.

Even the toy industry assaulted our moral foundations. In the early 1950's, a new toy captured the hearts of young American girls: the "Barbie Doll." This voluptuous doll brainwashed young girls by establishing an impossible and extremely physical standard of beauty for females.

Barbie somehow became the acceptable model for all that was desirable in American young women. Her artist-engineered body dimensions became the impossible norm for young girls: thin was in, fat was out. Beautiful was in, less than perfect was totally unacceptable. The Barbie Doll unconsciously launched a fashion revolution by reaching the nation's girls while they were young. By the 1960's, Barbie had a boyfriend called Ken, and countless young girls in the U.S. were aroused and stimulated into thinking, "I should have a boyfriend like Ken as well."

Love letters began to circulate in our schools. The situation has spiraled out of control, and today we have third graders writing love letters to one another and fifth graders are experimenting with sex!

Fashion and styles also influence the artificial romance and sexual stimulation of young men and young ladies. A young woman should always dress in feminine attire, but never sensuously. We should never allow the fashions of Hollywood to dictate the morality of our hearts.

Compare the statements you just read with these fashion fads from the past and present: the rise of mini-skirts; slit skirts; blouses that show cleavage, bare midriff designs featuring exposed belly buttons, low cut jeans, and g-string bathing suits. All of these demean the femininity of young women in America and throughout the world.

When you combine these provocative styles, standards, and fads with the enormously persuasive examples set by immoral celebrities, divas, entertainment industry idols, and big screen stars; you can readily see that we have problems. Young men, and especially young ladies, are easily influenced into a life style of premature romance and artificial love.

It is no wonder that in America and in most of the western world, it is almost expected for boys to have girlfriends and girls to have boyfriends. If you are 14 or 15 years old, you are expected to be going out with someone—at least to the school dance or prom.

Parents have been lulled into a spiritual stupor and an artificial sense of security. Many actually believe that their children will maintain their morality and virtue while going out on dates, coming back at all hours of the night, and spending time alone with a boyfriend or girlfriend in their rooms. This is virtually impossible.

The danger of Satan's Trojan horse is hidden for a good reason. He is perfectly content to allow the church to pray, preach, and witness as long as we allow our children to choose their spouses using this false American dating system. He counts on the fact that it circumvents and usurps the courtship and biblical process. The Word of God tells us in Romans 12:1-2 (NKJV):

> I beseech you, therefore, brethren by the mercies of God that you present your bodies a living sacrifice holy, acceptable to God, which is your reasonable service. And do not be conformed to this world, but be transformed by the renewing of your mind that you may prove what is that good and acceptable and perfect will of God.

Remember that your body (and the bodies of your children) is the temple of the Holy Spirit. In 1 Corinthians 6, we are commanded to glorify God in our bodies. With all the talk of sexual temptation nowadays, the first thing young people should do — and what parents should encourage constantly — is to present their bodies as a living

**1 Corinthians 6:20**
"For you were bought at a price; therefore glorify God in your body and in your spirit, which are God's."

sacrifice. In other words, give your body over to Jesus and die to inordinate and unscriptural passions.

As you begin to do this, Romans 12:2 (NKJV), begins to take effect: "And do not be conformed to this world." In other words, do not allow the music industry, motion picture industry, television programmers, peer pressure, and fashion designers into your life. Do not allow them to compel you to have a girlfriend or a boyfriend. That has never been God's plan for you.

This is God's plan: *When love begins to develop, it is time to get married.* He never intended for young people to "make out," touch each other inordinately and unscripturally, and then try to stop before having sexual intercourse.

God never intended for young people to experience all of the physical and emotional aspects of romance before marriage. We are not to be conformed to this world. We must save romance, true love, and sexual union for the guilt-free and blessed covenant of marriage.

We must return to the biblical standards of courtship and betrothal. Parents, *get involved.* If you don't have time, make time. It says in Romans 12:2 (NKJV), "But be transformed by the renewing of your mind." Allow the Holy Spirit to completely deprogram all of the brainwashing you have received in your life. Allow Him to make you immune to peer pressure!

If you decide to wait until marriage for true love (not just sex); if you decide to delay all interest in love and romance until the right one comes along, then you will suffer persecution. It is because you will be different from everyone else.

Even in Christian schools and in our churches, any young person who decides to wait for love must be prepared to be mocked, ostracized, and ridiculed. Be encouraged. Romans 12:2 (NKJV) goes on to say, "…that you may prove what is that good and acceptable and perfect will of God."

In other words, as you present your body a living sacrifice, God can (1) begin to break the power of the world's anti-Christian brainwashing; (2) strengthen you to return to biblical standards; and (3) give you the assurance that the one God brings to you as your perfect spouse is part of the "good, acceptable and perfect will of God" for you.

God's will should be confirmed by your parents and pastors. Here is a simple formula:

- Romans 12:1b is *dedication*: "...present your bodies a living sacrifice...."

- Romans 12:2a is *deprogramming*: "Do not be conformed to this world but be transformed by the renewing of your mind."

- Romans 12:2b is *discovery*: "... that you may prove what is the good and acceptable and perfect will of God."

This is the pattern and formula for knowing the person who is to be your spouse for life. Indeed, we can say that: *Dedication + Deprogramming = Discovery of God's Best for Your Life.*

# DISCUSSION GUIDE
## Questions for Parents and Young People

1.  What Trojan horse has Satan subtly placed within the walls of the home and the church?

2.  Why do you think people seldom heard of divorce or immorality in society while America and the western world practiced courtship?

3.  Explain the courtship process from beginning to end.

4.  How has technology contributed to premature romance and artificial love within society?

5. How has television affected the American family and the dating/going-out process?

6. How can fashion, idols, and divas affect young people?

7. How does peer pressure cause young people to make premature, romantic, and artificial love decisions?

PERFECTION
PEACE PURITY
PRESERVATION

## CHAPTER 12
## The Four P's

*"Now may the God of peace himself sanctify you completely; and may your whole spirit, soul, and body be preserved blameless at the coming of our Lord Jesus Christ." 1 Thessalonians 5:23 (NKJV)*

The above-mentioned scripture is one of the most outstanding verses in the New Testament. It not only describes the three components of man, but it also reveals four goals God the Father wants to accomplish in the life of every Christian before the coming of our Lord Jesus Christ.

### The Four Goals of God the Father

First of all, *the God of peace wants to present every believer in peace* before the coming of the Lord Jesus Christ. Concerning our topic, it is the will of God that every believer be at peace with human relationships—especially marriage relationships.

Secondly, *the God of purity* wants to *sanctify us* or set us apart. Our text says, "Now may the God of peace himself *sanctify you . . .*" I believe it is always the will of God for there to be sanctity or purity in our human relationships, friendships, love and romance. As mentioned before, awakening love and romance prematurely before one is ready for marriage makes it extremely difficult to maintain purity in the relationship.

Thirdly, *the God of perfection* wants every area of our being to be *completely sanctified* for the Lord Jesus Christ as indicated in the scripture—"Now may the God of peace himself sanctify you *completely. . ."*

Fourthly, *the God of preservation wants to preserve us.* The text says, "…and may your whole spirit, soul, and body be preserved blameless at the coming of the Lord Jesus Christ."

God the Father wishes to preserve three specific components of every Christian person—the spirit, the soul and the body. It is interesting to note that just as God is a Trinity or a tri-unity—God the Father, God the Son, and God the Holy Spirit—you also consist of three different components: spirit, soul, and body.

Just as there is one God in three persons—Father, Son, and Holy Spirit; so every individual consists of spirit, soul, and body. Just as the Father, Son, and Holy Spirit exist as one God and cannot be separated; neither can you separate any one of the three components of your makeup because you would cease to be yourself.

When it comes to the subject of love and marriage, we should realize that it involves *two* spirits, *two* souls, and *two* bodies coming together. It is the will of God for that sacred relationship to have peace, purity, perfection, and preservation. That is best accomplished as the Christian waits until he or she is *ready* for marriage before the arousal of love and romance.

## The Human Spirit

The spirit within you is that part of your being that makes you aware of God. The spirit includes something called the conscience which helps you to distinguish between right and wrong. It also has an area called communion which makes you aware of God and gives you a desire to communicate with Him. A third part of the human spirit is called creativity. This is what makes us different in the areas of preferences, desires, styles, likes and dislikes. Your creativity, for example, affects whether you like to work with your hands, want to be with people, or excel in artistic ability. A fourth area of the human spirit is called the temperament. It determines your God-given personality.

The Greeks determined there were four basic personality types. Although these are not mentioned specifically in the Bible, they are generally useful for understanding our personalities: (1) choleric—a dominant, forceful, "type A" personality; (2) sanguine—a happy go lucky, expressive and verbal personality; (3) phlegmatic—a laid-back personality; and (4) melancholic—a contemplative, detailed, artistic, musically-oriented personality.

The Apostle Paul, for example, seemed to exhibit a choleric personality. The Apostle Peter seems to have been a sanguine. Barnabas and Andrew had phlegmatic personalities and King David was a good example of a melancholic personality.

When you are born again, it is your spirit that is regenerated and revitalized. When God lives in you, He lives in your spirit. This is the most important and influential part of your being. As your spirit makes you aware of God, your soul makes you aware of yourself. The

Greek word for soul is *psuche*, and this is our source for the word, psychology. I've heard it said many times that the biblical word, soul, refers to your mind, your emotions, and your will. In other words, your soul determines the way you think, feel, and decide. This is the part of your being that you control. As the spirit must be released, the soul must be renewed as explained in Romans 12:1-2.

The third component of every human being is the physical body. It is the body that makes us aware of the world around us through our five physical senses—seeing, hearing, touching, feeling, and smelling. As the spirit must be released and the soul must be renewed, so must the body be restricted from its natural appetites, covetousness, and carnality. A great principal in life is that "the body is a wonderful servant but a horrible master." You and I cannot be led by the appetites and desires of our bodies.

## Alignment

Alignment refers to the state of a person whose three components are in proper balance. The spirit is the dominating part of his life. The soul is next in line, but in submission to the spirit. The body is in submission to both the spirit and soul (and in that order). This is the ideal alignment or balance

**Spirit**
↓
**Soul**
↓
**Body**

for a Christian's life. As described in 1 Thessalonians 5:23, alignment demonstrates that the whole *spirit*, *soul*, and *body* is being preserved blameless until Jesus comes.

## Arousal

> *"When we were controlled by our old nature,
> sinful desires were at work within us and the
> law aroused these evil desires that produce sinful
> deeds resulting in death...But sin took advantage
> of this law and aroused all kinds of forbidden
> desires within me. If there were no law, sin would
> not have that power"* (Romans 7:5,8 NKJV).

For our purpose as it relates to premature love and
romance, the *soul* is aroused by romantic and sensual
interest. This in turn begins to dominate and overpower
the influence of the *spirit*. The soul gradually begins
to exercise dominance over the influence of the young
person's spirit by the following seven steps:

*The first step is defrauding or flirting.* When young people
flirt, they draw attention to themselves and especially
to their physical bodies. Very often, they sexually excite
another young person. First Thessalonians 4:6 (NKJV) says,
"No one should take advantage of and defraud his brother
in this matter." This clearly applies to the process of
arousal, when a young girl wears provocative clothing and
acts in a flirtatious way to draw the attention of a young
man to herself physically. (A young man may just as easily
defraud a young lady through flirtatious ways.)

*The second step after defrauding is delight.* It is what
happens when a young man is delighted by what he sees
and is attracted to her. At this point, the sensual desire
called lust begins to increase.

*This takes us to the third step which is deception.* In deception,
a young person's human spirit begins to react to the
temptation by justifying the soul's cravings with excuses
such as, "It is normal," or "Everybody else is doing it."

*He quickly moves into step four—doubting.* The young man now must either admit that Scripture is absolute in his life, or, as so many before him have done, he begins to doubt Scripture. "There is nothing wrong with this feeling that I have," he tells himself. "I'm not so sure I believe in the Word of God anymore—not all of it anyway. I just don't interpret Scripture that way."

*This takes us to step five—disregard.* He begins to disregard his human conscience and choses to accept and reciprocate or give back in return the feelings of lust.

*Step number six is degradation.* At this state, the young man and young lady become an "item." They are officially viewed as a couple; they are going out with one another. They may have limited physical exchange at this point. In other words, they begin holding hands, light kisses, and hugging one another; thus defrauding and arousing themselves even more.

*Finally, they reach step seven—"misalignment."* Misalignment is best illustrated by the following chart:

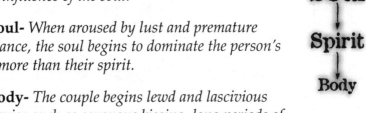

**Spirit-** *The spirit is now under the submission and influence of the soul.*

**Soul-** *When aroused by lust and premature romance, the soul begins to dominate the person's life more than their spirit.*

**Body-** *The couple begins lewd and lascivious behavior such as sensuous kissing, long periods of necking, fondling, etc.*

If the couple continues down the road of arousal, they will eventually wind up in what I call abnormality.

## Abnormality

> *"When they refused to acknowledge God, he abandoned them to their evil minds and let them do things that should never be done"* (Romans 1: 28, New Living Translation)

The King James Version calls the evil mind a "reprobate mind." A reprobate or evil mind is a mind that has lost or destroyed the ability to discern right from wrong, and good from evil. We see the beginnings of this demonic switch of good and evil in popular statements such as, "What's wrong with this. Everybody is doing it so why can't I?"

As Christians, we must remember that we are surrounded by reprobate thinking. The most vivid form of reprobate thinking and switched value systems appear in movies and television programs, because so many of them are based on opinions and lifestyles rooted in relativism where there is no absolute truth. Christians must remember that we must be holy because God commands it. We need young people who are strong enough to say no, and who will wait until the right time before they pursue love and romance. Again, the right time is the time when they are ready for marriage.

**Spirit-** *Unable to discern evil*

**Soul-** *The soul is now under the influence and submission to the body.*

**Body-** *The body influences and controls the motivations of the soul and spirit.*

**Body**
↓
**Soul**
↓
**Spirit**

# DISCUSSION GUIDE
## Questions for Parents and Young People

1. What are the three components of every human being?

2. What is the fourfold aim and goal of God the Father concerning your spirit, soul, and body?

3. What are the three components of the soul?

4. By using arrows, illustrate or describe a person who is in proper alignment.

5. Explain the seven-fold downward process of arousal.

6. Define the following: defrauding, lewdness, and lasciviousness.

7. Regarding abnormality, what is meant by an evil or reprobate mind?

# Chapter 13
# THREE BLIND MICE

*"And if the blind leads the blind, both will fall into a ditch"* (Matthew 15:14b, NKJV).

The warning of Jesus about "the blind leading the blind" reveals three startling insights:

**There is no sight—"and if the blind"**

**There is no sense—"leads the blind"**

**There is no safety—"both will fall into a ditch"**

This passage reveals a grave warning to every young person and their parents concerning premature love and romance in these last days. The prophet Hosea said in Hosea 4:6 (NKJV), "My people are destroyed for a lack of knowledge." And the writer of Proverbs tells us in Proverbs 29:18a (NKJV), "Where there is no revelation, the people cast off restraint." Before any young person even thinks about going out or pursuing romance, be aware that a lack of knowledge of God's principles and patterns can bring much destruction to your dreams, ambitions and innocence.

When it comes to the subject of love and romance, it seems there is no sight, no direction, and no clearcut revelation in the U.S. and in western Europe about the fact that *God never intended for romance or love to be pursued before the right time.*

Without revelation from God concerning love, romance, and the choice of a future spouse, we will see what happens when, as the prophet said, "the people cast off restraint." This means they will not inhibit or restrain their emotions, desires, and possibly even their sexual urges.

How can the blind lead the blind? How can people who have no sight even think about leading others who are blind? There is no sight and there is no sense because, as the Scripture says, "the blind lead the blind."

This is what we have in America today—a people with a temporal value system based on situation ethics and relativism who are blind to God's principles. Yet these people trust themselves to date and go out and actually choose a spouse on their own in spiritual darkness. It is no wonder that we have such a high divorce rates in western societies. We are a people with no sight, vision or revelation of God's principles doing the unthinkable—presuming to lead others into a premature path of romantic delusion and disillusionment.

Jesus said that *both* blind persons fell into a ditch. In America and Western Europe today, our marriages are quickly falling into the ditch of divorce. We have young people falling into the ditch of romantic disillusionment, and truly there is no safety in the American dating system.

The Apostle Paul gives us a very important principle that we need to consider in Colossians 2:8 (NKJV): "Beware lest anyone cheat you through philosophy and empty deceit, according to the tradition of men, according to the basic principles of the world, and not according to Christ."

In America today, there are four strong worldly philosophies or influences affecting young people and their parents with respect to premature love and romance:

## Myths

The first worldly influence may be called popular *myths* concerning dating or going out. There are four key myths to consider:

*Myth 1 – Dating/Going Out is a normal part of growing up.* The truth is that dating or going out is not normal. It promotes promiscuity and prepares young people for divorce as we saw in the earlier chapters. In addition, dating as a practice is a newcomer in the world social scene. Courtship and betrothal was practiced not only in the biblical world, but also in Africa, Asia, Europe, and in the U.S. until the early 20th century.

*Myth 2 — Dating/Going Out is the right process for selecting a future spouse.* In reality, courtship was the traditional method of choosing a future spouse. One of the great strengths of this system was that it included a very strong parental blessing.

*Myth 3 — A young person "comes of age" when they are aware of their sexuality and have romantic feelings.* This is false, since the true "coming of age" occurs when young people become aware of right and wrong and take responsibility for their actions, choices, and decisions. The popular Hollywood scenario in many movies describes "coming of age" as the day a young man or woman discovers the opposite sex (or, even worse, when they have sex for the first time).

*Myth 4—It is normal for boys and girls to not only like each other but to get involved romantically and even go out with each other.* The truth is that this behavior is acquired or learned from their parents, from friends, or from society. It reflects the anti-biblical thinking the Apostle Paul described in Colossians 2:8 (NKJV) as "…philosophy and empty deceit, according to the tradition of men, according to the basic principles of the world, and not according to Christ."

## Media

The twenty-first century is a high-tech world of advanced television, movies, DVD's, internet, and high-definition videos—all of which have a dramatic effect on a young person's sight, hearing, and emotions. Concrete thinkers, in particular, tend to imitate what they see on a screen. Most of the television sitcoms and many so-called family programs overemphasize sex, romance, and rebellious young people defying their parents to seek romantic adventures outside of the house. It seems that the clarion call of the main television networks is: "Sex and violence sell! Therefore, give them more sex and violence."

Two networks, in particular, are very popular with young people at this writing. One features a sitcom based on a dysfunctional preacher's family in which all of the siblings seem to be preoccupied with sex and romance. Two other top-rated adult drama programs have an extreme overemphasis on sexuality and false romance—and they have a dramatic effect on the young people of America.

One of the networks produces popular sarcastically animated programs that consistently devalue the Word of God and promote disrespect, rebellion, and premature romance. I could hardly believe my eyes while channel surfing last year. I ran across an advertisement for an up and coming new program in which the character, a young teenage boy, is paddling in a canoe at camp when he sees teenage girls' bathing suits floating down the river. This was presented as a clear indication that they wanted to have sex with him.

Not only are the majority of PG-13 movies filled with sexual connotations, but PG movies and even some of the G movies send strong messages that it is okay to have a boyfriend or girlfriend at an early age.

## Music

Music is one of the most powerful influences affecting young people today. Parents need to know what their youngsters are listening to because there is a great deal of sensuality in the words and sounds of many modern music forms. I encourage all parents to sit down with their youngsters, write down the lyrics of the music, and have them repeat those lyrics to you. Then ask them, "Do these words reflect Christian values? Do the words reinforce scriptural standards? If the answer is no, perhaps you need to consider another music selection."

Teach them that the lifestyle of the artist is just as important as the lyrics on their albums. Is the artist promoting Christian values, or is the artist's work promoting hedonism—the doctrine that we are to live mainly for pleasure?

Moreover, please consider what many would consider an "innocent school dance." Dancing and choreography, in particular, promote vanity. When a young person does not know the steps, he or she is "out of it" while those who do are "in."

Dancing can also promote sensuality and promiscuity. When young people dance with one another, it is very possible that their movements may defraud a young man or young woman when they watch someone gyrating in front of them. (This is especially true when the partners hold and squeeze one another. Dancing, when combined with the sensuality of the music and lyrics, can be highly provocative. It may lead to sexual stimulation and even promiscuity.

Dancing and music were created for the Lord, but somehow Satan has perverted it as we see in Exodus 32. When Moses delayed coming down from the mountain, the Bible tells us in Exodus 32:6 that the people sat down to eat and drink, and then they "rose up to play" (the New Living Translation says they "indulged themselves in pagan revelry"). Verse 19 tells us that as soon as Moses came near the camp, "he saw the calf and the dancing." According to Exodus 25: 25 (NKJV), "...Moses saw that the people were unrestrained (for Aaron had not restrained them) to their shame among their enemies." (The term, "unrestrained," means the people had taken off their clothes.)

When God delayed Moses on the mountain, the Israelites at the foot of the mountain began to pick up the instruments they had received from Egypt and began to entertain themselves with music. It seems this quickly led to unrestrained lustful feelings. The implication here is that the Israelites engaged in public adultery and fornication on a mass scale. *I am not saying that all dancing is evil or sensuous*—I am only warning parents and young people to be very careful. Ask yourself these questions: Does the dancing and the music lead to sensuality? Does the dancing and music lead to premature feelings of romance and the desire to go out or date one another?

## Models

What type of role models does the world offer for our young people to follow? Our young people are making idols of the celebrities, divas, and stars they see on television and in the movies. These highly visible people have a deep influence on the future desires of our children for premature romance.

I get very concerned when I see a beautiful young singer who claims to be a Christian, yet she dresses provocatively and influences nine-year-old girls to dress the same way.

The stars of today (whether or not they are Christian artists or performers) influence many young ladies to dress provocatively in the name of style and fashion. Hollywood has a long history of immersion in high immorality, promiscuity, and a lack of loyalty and commitment to the marriage covenant. It's endless string of movie and television products often send wrong messages to this generation of young people.

Parents, do you have the final say over whom your young lady admires and whom your young man is watching? Do you have the final say on what they wear? (Final approval of shopping choices should rest with the parent, not the youngster.)

Young women need godly models who will teach them to be discreet and feminine rather than sensual and promiscuous. The best models are usually right in the home, and these mothers, aunts, grandmothers, and older sisters far outshine the questionable "stars" of today whose ungodly lives inflict countless scars in the young people who blindly emulate their every move (and sin).

# DISCUSSION GUIDE
## Questions for Parents and Young People

1. What is the common definition of "coming of age" and what is the scriptural definition?

2. Is it really normal for boys and girls to like each other and go out with one another? Or is this the result of learned deceptive behavior from other sources?

3. Name three television programs that are sexually explicit and explain how they present a view of premature romantic dating:

4. Name three movies that promote dating or going out at a young age, and explain how they do it:

5. Why do you think concrete thinkers tend to imitate what they see on the screen?

6. Who are your favorite musical artists? Do their lyrics and lifestyles reflect Christian values and Bible standards? Give examples.

7. Do you allow your parents to have the final say on the clothes you purchase and wear?

8. Name three of your favorite celebrities, and discuss the influence they have on your fashions, behavior, and beliefs about dating or going out.

# Chapter 14
# Spiritual Surgery

*"And if your right eye causes you to sin, pluck it out and cast it from you for it is more profitable for you that one of your members perish than for your whole body to be cast into hell. And if your right hand causes you to sin, cut it off and cast it from you, for it is more profitable for you that one of your members perish than for your whole body to be cast into hell"* Matthew 5:29-39, (NKJV).

God is speaking prophetically to His people all over the world. One of His main messages is this: We must return to biblical standards of courtship in our attempts to find a husband or wife. The seemingly endless cycle of divorce and fornication must *first* stop in the body of Christ. We simply cannot go on the way we are now or we will enter into a divorce rate of 60% and even 70% in the twenty-first century! For the Church to survive and to remain strong, we must hear God's clarion call to holiness and purity in our relationships and friendships. God is calling for parents, in particular, to wake up and come out of the slumber that has lulled them into a deceptive passivity. It causes them to sit back and allow their sons and daughters to date indiscriminately. It is a parent's responsibility to enforce biblical principles of love and courtship.

Jesus talked about severing anything, anyone, or any practice that is ungodly. This is a call to spiritual surgery. I call you, in the name of Jesus Christ, to sever the following ten things:

1. *Break-up all current boyfriend/girlfriend relationships.* Redefine the relationship as a friendship and determine to allow holiness and righteousness to prevail in that relationship. In other words, no more making out, fornication, or any kind of physical interaction that might be considered defrauding or promiscuous.

2. *Rededicate your life with all of your heart to the Lord Jesus Christ.* Repent of every sin you know of and determine to love Jesus with all your heart, soul, strength and mind (see Matthew 22:37). Put Jesus first in everything you do. Seek Him first and make Him the number one priority of your life. Matthew 6:33.

3. *Determine to wait for Jesus and trust Him to select for you a husband or wife.* If you indeed trust God with your salvation and trust His sovereignty for everything else, determine to allow Him the sovereignty of choosing a husband or wife (and to confirm His choice for you through your parents and pastors).

4. *Determine by the grace of God that you will not go out or date anyone until there is a strong witness* in your heart and with your parents and pastors that this young man or woman is your future husband or wife.

5. *Determine to adopt courtship principles when God shows you your future spouse.* Wait on the Lord until the right time. That will be when you are both mature emotionally, financially and spiritually (and when you have the blessing of both sets of parents and pastors).

6. *Separate from peers who pressure you.* Do not allow anyone in your life who tries to advise, manipulate or intimidate you to adopt a lifestyle, or to make decisions that are opposed to God's Word and godly patterns.

7. *Eliminate TV programs, movies, and videos that have sexual content.*

8. *Determine not to dress promiscuously or sensuously.*

9. *Eliminate music in which the lyrics and lifestyle of the artist emphasize sexuality and contradict God's Word.*

10. *Eliminate rebellion and pride from your life.* Remember the principle that "to the degree that you submit to the God-given authorities over your life, so will God give you protection over your life." Remember James 4:6 (NKJV) also: "God resists the proud and gives grace to the humble." Determine to walk in submission and humility and God will bless you.

# Projects for Chapter 14

1. Ask your parents to forgive you and be reconciled to them, especially if you have been rebellious against their authority.

2. Seek and utilize the help of your parents and/ or pastors to break-up all current boyfriend/ girlfriend relationships.

3. Go over your entire wardrobe and remove anything of a sensual or revealing nature.

4. Set aside a time for prayer and fasting and consecrate yourself to Jesus.

5. Go to your Christian bookstore and purchase some books on courtship. I would suggest that you read, *I Kissed Dating Good-bye* by Joshua Harris and *Choosing God's Best* by Dr. Don Rauniker.

# Chapter 15
# Going Out with Jesus

Every young person will eventually reach the age when curiosity for the opposite sex comes alive. As we noted earlier, the world calls this "coming of age." I believe the Bible calls this period "the difficult years." Ecclesiastes 12: 1 (NKJV) says, "Remember now your creator in the days of your youth before the difficult days come when the years draw near when you say I have no pleasure in them." When the time comes that young people have a desire to awaken love and passion in their lives, a critical decision must be made that will forever affect their lives on earth and their destiny in the hereafter.

The decision is this: *Do I allow another guy or girl to awaken my love and passion, or do I allow my passion and love for God to awaken?* The choice has to be made between these two types of love. For the time will come when one must choose between one or the other. Luke 16:13 says, "No servant can serve two masters for either he will hate the one and love the other or else he will be loyal to the one and despise the other." (NKJV) While the immediate context of this passage concerns money, it truly applies to the matter of love and romance. Simply put, you cannot serve the love interest of two people at the same time. You will either serve one with all your heart and despise the other or serve the other with all your heart and be disloyal to the first.

Parents, if young people allow their romantic love to awaken prematurely, they can expect to experience most if not all of the frustrations and pain described in this book. Yet, if they awaken their love and passion for God, they can look forward to years of purpose, destiny, and fulfillment.

I challenge you to "love not the world" or to be like it. Remember, all the world has to offer is the lust of the flesh, the lust of the eyes, and the pride of life (see 1 John 2:15-16). This passage accurately describes modern society with its premature arousal of love and romance.

Take the challenge to love Jesus with all of your heart, all of your soul, all of your strength and all of your mind as we are commanded in Matthew 22:37-38. If you feel you must date or go out with somebody, then I strongly encourage you to go out with Jesus and be faithful and loyal to Him. If we're going to make Jesus our first love in life; and if we're going to "go out with Jesus," we must first realize how much He loves us. We read in the Psalms:

> I will praise you for I am fearfully and wonderfully made; marvelous are your works and that my soul knows very well. My frame was not hidden from you when I was made in secret and skillfully wrought in the lowest parts of the earth. Your eyes saw my substance being yet unformed and in your book they all were written. The days fashioned for me when as yet they were none of them. How precious are your thoughts to me Oh God! How great is the sum of them! If I should count them they would be more in number than the sand. When I

awake I am still with you (Psalms 139:14-18, NKJV).

We need to realize how much God loved us and that He *initiated* that love. 1 John 4:19 (NKJV) tells us, "We love Him because He first loved us." Going out with Jesus is simply accepting His invitation to be your closest friend and to be the lover of your soul. Going out with Jesus involves spending time with Him, so it is critical that you spend quality time in devotions, daily prayer, fasting, and in the study of the Word of God. This involves intimacy in praise and worship and in your daily walk with God.

Going out with Jesus implies that you should pledge your loyalty and dedication to Him and Him alone. It means you are not to let down your guard. Guard the intimacy and love relationship that you have with Jesus, and guard your heart so you will not lose your first love (see Revelation 2:4).

Exercise great caution with friendships because friends can influence you away from your love, passion, and commitment to God. Also, be careful with what you desire because your desires often determine your decisions. Your decisions can often determine whether or not Jesus Christ remains your first love.

Music is also a key factor in romantic relationships. Many couples consistently want to hear and dance to music. You must make wise choices in your music because the music you allow in your spirit may directly determine your intimacy level with Jesus Christ.

In my opinion, God wants us to primarily listen to praise and worship music—or music with lyrics that will never contradict the Word of God written and performed by an artist whose lifestyle exemplifies Jesus. I base this on Paul's admonition to the Philippians:

> Finally, brethren, whatever things are true, whatever things are noble, whatever things are just, whatever things are pure, whatever things are lovely, whatever things are of good report, if there is any virtue and if there is anything praiseworthy; meditate on these things (Philippians 4:8, NKJV).

Be careful to guard the "gate" of your ears and eyes when it comes to the entertainment you choose. It will have a definite effect on your love and passion for Jesus.

Finally, if you love Jesus with all of your heart and if He is truly the first love of your life, then you will develop a relationship of trust with Him.

You have already trusted Jesus with your salvation. (We are saved by grace and faith through the blood of Jesus according to Ephesians 2:8.) Now you must trust Him with your future, with your destiny, with your plans, and with whatever He allows in your life. Trust Him, knowing that all things work together for good to them that love God who are called according to His purpose (see Romans 8:28).

Allow Jesus to make the choice of your future husband or wife. Show Him how much you love Him choosing His way instead of the world's destructive method of dating and going out.

# Parental Prayer:

Heavenly Father, with all my heart I come to You. I commit myself to be transparent with my son/daughter. I must have integrity: when I am wrong I must say I am wrong and repent. I commit to You this night to do my utmost to build the bonds of love with my children and spouse. I commit to You that I will have daily devotions with You and endeavor to do my best to have devotions with my family. Help me to let you guide and control my life. Help me not to judge. Help me to discern and give me patience. Let the fruit of the Spirit be prevalent in my ministry as a parent. I want to mold a man or woman of God. Please give me Your strength and give me mercy for the mistakes I will make. Give me grace for the mistakes I have already made. I commit to being a godly parent. Grant me great favor in the eyes of my children. I commit this to You this _____ day of _____, _____, in Jesus' name.                              (month)       (year)

# Teenage Prayer:

Lord Jesus Christ, on this day I come to You desiring to stand as a man or woman of God. Help me during these critical teenage years with all of these fluctuations in my emotions. I put my trust in You. You, Lord, have given me the parents You saw fit for me to have. You have given me the home in which You placed me, and I want to thank You for it. I commit to You this day that I will be a grateful son/daughter to my father and mother. Lord I willingly submit myself to parental and pastoral authority, and to other authorities You have established; knowing that I cannot trust the variations in my life. Help the authorities over me to be used by You to help mold me and shape me into the person You have called me to be. Help me to flee youthful lusts and to not be deceived or ensnared by the devil. Build bridges of communication and a bond of love with my parents. Let there be trust, respect and love in my home. I ask You, Father, to use my authorities to train me to be a man/woman of God. Let rebellion and immorality be far from me. I present all of my friends to You, God. Let me be a living witness to them that they may see Christ in me and have a chance to be saved. I commit this to You this _____ day of _____, _____, in Jesus' name.
                        (month)            (year)

# Chapter 16
# Is It Too Late For Me?

Deep sadness and regret grip many of the young people who hear the Bible principles presented in this book. *"It is too late for me,"* they tell themselves. *"I've already sinned. I lost my virginity last year on prom night. Now I feel trapped by friends who expect me to continue with a loose lifestyle. What use does God have for me now?"*

God has Good News for you if you are one of the countless young people in junior high school, high school, or college, who fell into sin through promiscuous sexual activity.

One young woman was caught in the act of adultery by religious leaders and dragged in front of Jesus. The Jewish laws of that day were very strict, and the woman's captors wanted to see if Jesus would dismiss the law or command that the woman be stoned to death by the crowd as the law allowed.

Jesus knows the hearts of men and women. I am sure He observed that only one adulterer was brought before Him. It seems the man involved had conveniently been permitted to escape. How did the Son of God treat this woman who was obviously guilty of sexual sin?

[The scribes and Pharisees] said to Him, "Teacher, this woman was caught in adultery, in the very act. "Now Moses, in the law, commanded us that such should be stoned. But what do You say?" This they said, testing Him, that they might have something of which to accuse Him. But Jesus stooped down and wrote on the ground with His finger, as though He did not hear. So when they continued asking Him, He raised Himself up and said to them, *"He who is without sin among you, let him throw a stone at her first."* And again He stooped down and wrote on the ground. Then those who heard it, being convicted by their conscience, went out one by one, beginning with the oldest even to the last. And Jesus was left alone, and the woman standing in the midst. When Jesus had raised Himself up and saw no one but the woman, He said to her, "Woman, where are those accusers of yours? Has no one condemned you?" She said, "No one, Lord." And Jesus said to her, *"Neither do I condemn you; go and sin no more"* (John 8: 4-11, emphasis mine, NKJV).

Jesus did not condemn this woman, nor did He condone her sin or release her to continue in her sin. I am convinced that Jesus perceived what the woman's accusers refused to see or accept that this young woman had *genuinely repented of her sin.*

Jesus Christ possessed the right and the authority to condemn the woman but He extended God's mercy instead. He also had the power to forgive sins, and He freely forgave her.

Many years later the Holy Spirit inspired John the apostle to write these words to real-life Christians who were struggling with past sins and daily failures:

*If we confess our sins, He is faithful and just to forgive us our sins and to cleanse us from all unrighteousness.* If we say that we have not sinned, we make Him a liar, and His word is not in us. My little children, these things I write to you, so that you may not sin. And if anyone sins, we have an Advocate with the Father, Jesus Christ the righteous" (1 John 1:9—2:1, emphasis mine, NKJV).

These promises of God delivered through the apostle John should give all of us great hope. This Bible passage lays out a roadmap to recovery and a new life in Jesus Christ for anyone who has failed and fallen into sexual sin.

If you fall into this category, the first door is for *you* to open. It is called "confession of sin." Admit to Him what you have done and turn away from your sin with all of your heart. Then God Himself will step in because He is faithful in His love and perfectly just in His ways.

The Bible says Jesus, your heavenly lawyer and defender, your personal Advocate, intercedes before the Court of God. When He pleads your case, your *sins* will be forgiven and *you* will be cleansed of all unrighteousness! In other words, you get a fresh start, a new beginning, a second chance!

Compassionate Christian workers have rescued multiplied thousands of unwed young teenage women who found themselves pregnant and alone. Urged by many to take the easy way out and abort the innocent babies in their wombs, they chose life and discovered the compassion and forgiveness that can only be found in Jesus Christ.

This is the *only* Christ-like response to young people who have sinned and made mistakes and now seek forgiveness.

If you have already crossed the line and become sexually active, it isn't too late for you to *stop* and ask God for a fresh start.

Begin by turning away from sin right now. Confess your sins to Jesus Christ and ask Him for forgiveness. Allow Him to cleanse you from your sin.

The next step—especially if you are pregnant—is to find godly Christ-centered counselors and mentors who will stand alongside you throughout your pregnancy. Your pastor, other proven leaders in your church, or Christian workers from a "pro-life" pregnancy crisis center may help you reconcile with your parents if necessary. They will also help find proper medical care for you. They offer compassionate Bible-based counsel and assistance that can make all of the difference in your pregnancy, delivery, and afterward.

One of the greatest dangers you will face as a Christian young person who has been sexually active is *the temptation to resume your sinful lifestyle.* Even though your sin has been forgiven and forgotten in the eyes of God, you still have some "mind and soul rehabilitation" ahead of you.

Things get far more difficult once your God-given love has been "awakened before the time" outside of marriage. Again, there is great hope. We all come to Christ in a sinful condition, and we all must become "new creatures" through regeneration according to 2 Corinthians 5:17.

As we read earlier, John said, "If we confess our sins, he is faithful and just to forgive us our sins, and to cleanse us from all unrighteousness" (1 John 1:9, NKJV). God will cleanse you of all unrighteousness if you turn to Him with all of your heart.

The next step is to begin all over again at chapter 1 of this book and follow the biblical principles presented in this book to reform your belief system, lifestyle, thinking patterns, and relationships *God's way.*

Once you confess your sins and receive a fresh start in Jesus, it is important to *live* God's way. Any shortcuts, detours, or wandering will only lead you back to sin.

Remember the words of Jesus to the woman caught in the very act of sexual sin: "Go and sin no more." God is merciful and gracious, but He cannot be fooled. The Bible says He knows the very thoughts and intents of the heart (see Hebrews 4:12). Don't try to "deceive" God—He cannot be deceived or put off.

If you really want a fresh start, then begin a fresh relationship with God marked by total honesty and transparency. If you only want to avoid "getting caught," then there is very little I or anyone else can do for you (even the hands of God may be "tied" by this kind of attitude).

## A Special Note to Parents

If you are the parent of a teenager who has already stepped into sexual promiscuity, I want to encourage you as well. If your daughter comes to you in tears to announce that she is pregnant, I urge you not to reject her or lash out at her in anger. She needs your love and support now more than ever before.

You may find yourself on the other side of the equation with a son who has fathered a child out of wedlock. Again, let your first reaction follow the pattern of Jesus' reaction to the young woman caught in adultery. Your son probably already knows that what he did was wrong. Now he needs your help to make wise decisions and to approach the future with greater responsibility.

The first step, if possible, is to accompany him as he confesses his sin to the young lady's parents. Then you can provide invaluable help as you work with the other set of parents to determine the will of God for your children and for the baby that is on the way. It is not my purpose in this book to provide detailed counsel in this area, but I would like to direct you to those who will. Contact the nearest Christ-centered crisis pregnancy center and accompany both young people to consult with counselors there.

Very often it is not wise for unwed parents to marry—the immaturity, poor financial base, and incomplete education they bring to the marriage may well help doom them to lives of poverty and unhappiness. Abortion is not a biblical option, but there are many childless couples of high integrity and Christian morals who are desperate to locate and legally adopt children to raise as their own.

Many crisis pregnancy centers have funds set aside to provide high quality medical care, maternity housing, and godly support for unwed mothers. They also provide invaluable biblical training to help reshape any cracked or missing moral underpinnings so that these young women can make a fresh start in life.

Sexual intercourse outside of marriage and unwed parenthood are serious sins to be avoided; but if you or your children commit a sexual sin and pregnancy occurs, life has not ended. Yes, it will be much more complex and difficult, but God is gracious and full of compassion for those who repent and turn away from their ungodly lifestyles. There is hope in Christ!